Library Support for Study Abroad

SPEC Kits

Supporting Effective Library Management for Over Thirty Years

Committed to assisting research and academic libraries in the continuous improvement of management systems, ARL has worked since 1970 to gather and disseminate the best practices for library needs. As part of its committment, ARL maintains an active publications program best known for its SPEC Kits. Through the Collaborative Research/Writing Program, librarians work with ARL staff to design SPEC surveys and write publications. Originally established as an information source for ARL member libraries, the SPEC series has grown to serve the needs of the library community worldwide.

What are SPEC Kits?

Published six times per year, SPEC Kits contain the most valuable, up-to-date information on the latest issues of concern to libraries and librarians today. They are the result of a systematic survey of ARL member libraries on a particular topic related to current practice in the field. Each SPEC Kit contains an executive summary of the survey results; survey questions with tallies and selected comments; the best representative documents from survey participants, such as policies, procedures, handbooks, guidelines, Web sites, records, brochures, and statements; and a selected reading list—both print and online sources— containing the most current literature available on the topic for further study.

Subscribe to SPEC Kits

Subscribers tell us that the information contained in SPEC Kits is valuable to a variety of users, both inside and outside the library. SPEC Kit purchasers use the documentation found in SPEC Kits as a point of departure for research and problem solving because they lend immediate authority to proposals and set standards for designing programs or writing procedure statements. SPEC Kits also function as an important reference tool for library administrators, staff, students, and professionals in allied disciplines who may not have access to this kind of information.

SPEC Kits can be ordered directly from the ARL Publications Distribution Center. To order, call **(301) 362-8196**, fax **(301) 206-9789**, e-mail **pubs@arl.org**, or go to **http://www.arl.org/resources/pubs/**.

Information on SPEC Kits and the SPEC survey program can be found at **http://www.arl.org/resources/ pubs/spec/index.shtml**. The executive summary for each kit after December 1993 can be accessed free of charge at **http://www.arl.org/resources/pubs/spec/complete.shtml**.

SPEC Kit 309

Library Support for Study Abroad
December 2008

Ann Lindell

Head, Architecture & Fine Arts Library

University of Florida

ASSOCIATION OF RESEARCH LIBRARIES

Series Editor: Lee Anne George

SPEC Kits are published by the

Association of Research Libraries
21 Dupont Circle, NW, Suite 800
Washington, DC 20036-1118
P (202) 296-2296 F (202) 872-0884
http://www.arl.org/resources/pubs/spec/
pubs@arl.org

ISSN 0160 3582

ISBN 1-59407-808-4
978-1-59407-808-8

Copyright © 2008

SPEC Kit 309

Library Support for Study Abroad

December 2008

SURVEY RESULTS

REPRESENTATIVE DOCUMENTS

Library Services for Study Abroad Programs

SELECTED RESOURCES

SURVEY RESULTS

EXECUTIVE SUMMARY

Introduction

Research universities have long supported study abroad programs of varying nature, including short-term study tours and service learning experiences, as well as semester- and year-long academic programs. For this survey, "study abroad program" was broadly defined as a short-term, formal, credit-bearing educational program taking place outside of the country of the home institution. As society becomes more globally focused, and industry requires workers who are prepared to work in a multinational environment, these programs are becoming more critical to America's competitiveness.

Providing research materials and library services targeted to participants in these programs is a particular challenge. This survey was designed to explore how ARL member libraries are responding to the needs of faculty and student participants in various types of study abroad programs. It explored which library services and resources are provided to participants, how library support is staffed and administered, whether collections are physical or online, and how services are delivered.

The survey was distributed to the 123 ARL member libraries in May 2008. Fifty-three libraries completed the survey by the deadline of June 27 for a 43% response rate. Forty-four of the respondents (83%) reported that their university sponsors study abroad programs. The number of programs per institution ranges from as few as two to as many as 1200, with an average of 141 and a median of 50. At 26 institutions, study abroad programs receive library support, at

12 they do not. Four respondents did not supply this data, though one explained, "The programs don't receive library support but the individual students are supported." The 12 respondents from libraries that do not support study abroad programs submitted the survey at this point.

Description of Study Abroad Program

The remaining 32 respondents were asked to select one representative program and describe its location, subjects offered, duration, and number of students and faculty. Some described the overall program. Not surprisingly, programs are located around the world and cover a full range of disciplines. They vary in length from a few weeks to a semester to a year or more. The number of students ranges from a handful to over a thousand. The number of faculty is proportional to the number of students and subjects offered, with as few as one and as many as 68 faculty spread across a number of locations.

Half of the programs are at a campus that is administered by a partner host institution. Only three are at a campus that is administered by the home institution. Others are in rented spaces, field stations or, in the case of the Semester at Sea, on a ship.

Library Support Provided to Study Abroad Program

All of the responding libraries report that students and faculty have remote access to online resources through the home institution in North America. Twenty-three (74%) report that employees at the home institution in North America provide library services remotely. Slightly fewer than half also rely on a host partner for access to physical and online resources and staff to provide services. Only nine home institutions provide collections at the study abroad site and only five of those have staff who provide services. In open-ended comments, several respondents reiterated that students and faculty with a valid ID and an Internet connection have access to all the same online resources and services wherever they are located.

Administration of Library Support for Study Abroad Program

In all but one case, the library at the home institution administers library support for students and faculty in study abroad programs. In the other case, the host institution administers support. In a third of the programs, administration is shared between the home and host libraries. In a few cases, the home library partners with a study abroad or distance education office or an academic department at the home institution.

About a third of the programs have a single individual who has administrative responsibility for library support services. Half of these individuals have a title that includes some variation of distance education. Others are reference or area studies librarians, or manage public or access services or a branch library.

The other two-thirds of the respondents described library support for study abroad along the lines of the following: "Services to all students at a distance are built into existing services: ILL, e-reference, and access to online resources."

Funding of Library Support for Study Abroad Program

A majority of respondents (22 or 71%) report that funding for these library services comes from the home library's general, acquisitions, and/or personnel budgets. Or as one respondent commented, "This work is absorbed into regular collections and services." A few libraries also receive some funds from the home or host institution or student fees. Only

two libraries report that they receive funds from a separate institutional budget for the study abroad program.

Study Abroad Program Library

If employees of the home institution provide library services and access to library resources in a physical location at the study abroad site, respondents were asked to answer questions about the collections, equipment, and staff in that facility. There were five responses.

Collections

These five collections include books, journals, AV materials, maps, and reference works. The number of items ranges from just over 100 to 12,000. All five respondents report that the collection is catalogued and searchable as a discreet collection, though only three say the materials are included and searchable in the home library OPAC. Circulation policies are similar to the home library's.

Equipment and Staffing

All of the libraries provide desktop computers and printers. Since most students bring their own laptops, two provide wireless Internet access and only one has a loaner laptop. Four have photocopiers but only two have scanners. Two provide video equipment. Three of the libraries are staffed by one non-librarian professional, two of whom work full-time. A fourth has one librarian and two additional support staff. The fifth is staffed by two librarians and a few student assistants.

Library Services for the Study Abroad Program

In addition to the online resources that are available to all students and faculty who have a valid ID and Internet connection, study abroad participants also receive a range of library services. All but one of the 30 responding libraries offer reference service; the other only offers document delivery. Eleven libraries offer a combination of reference, ILL and/or document delivery, and instruction. Ten others offer at least reference and ILL or document delivery.

Reference and instruction services are largely delivered by library staff at the home library via e-mail, chat/instant messaging, or phone. Eleven respondents report they are delivering resource guides and tutorials online using such tools as Libguides, Camtasia, Captivate, and Searchpath. Eight communicate with students, whether studying abroad or not, by means of blogs, wikis, and Facebook.

All but two of the home libraries deliver electronic materials directly to study abroad students and faculty; half of the 28 respondents will also deliver hard copy directly to students and faculty. A few send materials to the onsite library instead.

Challenges of Library Support for Study Abroad Programs

Twenty-four respondents described one or more challenges the library faces in providing support for study abroad programs. Several categories emerged, as represented by the comments below.

ILL/DD: "Costs and security of delivering hard copy library materials. Institutional/policy constraints to providing document delivery to students."

Acquisitions: "Materials ordered by the home institution are shipped directly to the study abroad location. It can be difficult to verify receipt of materials for which we are invoiced."

Awareness: "We suspect that many Study Abroad students are unaware that they are eligible to continue receiving full library services while they are away."

Time zones: "Time differential in providing reference services such as IM/Chat which is not provided at the home institution on a 24/7 basis."

Cooperation: "Engaging faculty in a serious cooperative effort geared towards the selection and provision of library resources."

Internet access: "While we assert that study abroad participants have the same access to e-library collections and services that our local users enjoy (as long as they authenticate via a proxy server), the reality may be that hardware, software, and network/bandwidth issues abroad may severely limit that access, or make it impracticable."

Number of programs: "It's difficult to keep up with the ever-increasing number and variety of study abroad opportunities on this campus, therefore difficult to know how well we're meeting needs."

Changes Over Time

The survey asked whether the number of study abroad programs—and the number that receive library support—had increased, decreased, or stayed about the same in the previous five years. The majority (20 of 28 or 71%) report that both the number of programs and the number that receive library support increased. Seven report that those numbers have stayed about the same. Only one reports they have decreased. Eighteen respondents anticipate that the number of study abroad programs will increase in the coming five years and most will increase library support. Eight libraries expect that the number of programs and library support will stay about the same in the near future.

Conclusion

A comment from one survey respondent summarizes the current level of library support for study abroad students and faculty at ARL member institutions, "We do not have any particular initiatives aimed at study abroad participants. We have a large number of distance students (remote users) to begin with and we provide the same level of support for study abroad students as we do for distance students. At this point we are not sure that the students heading off to study abroad programs know that the services we have for distance users apply to them. Anecdotally, we do get feedback every semester from students who go abroad and tell us that their access to our library's databases and full-text journals was a lifesaver."

According to the Institute of International Education's most recent data, over 223,000 US students annually study abroad for academic credit. While this is a small percent of the total student population, IIE's annual survey of student mobility shows steady growth since 1985 and there are widespread calls to double, triple or even quadruple the number of participants in the coming decade.

Congress is pushing forward with the Senator Paul Simon Study Abroad Foundation Act that establishes the recommendations put forth by the Commission on the Abraham Lincoln Study Abroad Fellowship Program. This legislation creates a national program that will establish study abroad as the norm, not the exception, for undergraduate students. It would use leveraged grants to increase the number of American students who study abroad to one million annually within a decade.

As the number of study abroad participants grows, ARL Member libraries will be well positioned to serve these and other remotely located students through their increasingly digital libraries.

SURVEY QUESTIONS AND RESPONSES

The SPEC survey on Library Support for Study Abroad was designed by **Ann Lindell**, Head, Architecture & Fine Arts Library, University of Florida. These results are based on data submitted by 53 of the 123 ARL member libraries (43%) by the deadline of June 27, 2008. The survey's introductory text and questions are reproduced below, followed by the response data and selected comments from the respondents.

Research universities have long supported study abroad programs of varying nature, including short-term study tours and service learning experiences, as well as semester- and year-long academic programs. As society becomes more globally focused, and industry requires workers who are prepared to work in a multinational environment, these programs are becoming more critical to America's competitiveness.

According to the Institute of International Education's most recent data, over 223,000 US students annually study abroad for academic credit. While this is a small percent of the total student population, IIE's annual survey of student mobility shows steady growth since 1985 and there are widespread calls to double, triple or even quadruple the number of participants in the coming decade. Congress is pushing forward with the Senator Paul Simon Study Abroad Foundation Act that establishes the recommendations put forth by the Commission on the Abraham Lincoln Study Abroad Fellowship Program. This legislation creates a national program that will establish study abroad as the norm, not the exception, for undergraduate students. It would use leveraged grants to increase the number of American students who study abroad to one million annually within a decade. The bill has passed the House of Representatives and awaits approval from the Senate, where it has strong bipartisan support.

Study abroad programs are often now integral to degree programs across the academic disciplines, incorporating increasingly rigorous research components. Providing research materials and library services targeted to participants in these programs is a particular challenge. This survey is designed to explore how ARL member libraries are responding to the needs of faculty and student participants in various types of study abroad programs. It explores which library services and resources are provided to participants, how library support is staffed and administered, whether collections are physical or online, how services are delivered, etc. It strives to identify the challenges inherent in serving these constituencies, and to highlight innovative solutions to these challenges.

For the purpose of this survey, "study abroad program" is broadly defined as a short-term, formal, credit-bearing educational program taking place outside of the country of the home institution.

BACKGROUND

1. Does your university/institution sponsor study abroad programs? N=53

Yes	44	83%
No	7	13%
Not applicable, we are not an academic institution	2	4%

Comments

"In FY 2008, the University sponsored approximately 275 study abroad programs, including exchanges, semester programs, and short-term programs. Students can also participate in the literally thousands of non-university programs that are available as well as doing direct enrollment at overseas institutions."

"Mostly consists of exchange programs. Students will study abroad for 1 or 2 sessions as part of those programs. Libraries do not offer specific services to study abroad programs but this is partly because all of our students, whether they are at home or abroad, have access to our online collection and to reference services via e-mail. They are also considered registered students at the university abroad where they study so can take advantages of its library services, too."

"Our replies will be of a general nature regarding library services. No specific program is identified."

"Study abroad students have all the library use rights of university students, and have only logistical obstacles to overcome in using the library's resources. If they have Internet access they can authenticate and use our electronic resources, and Access Services will send them resources if they are requested. We do not however have a 'formal' support program. Theoretically, therefore, all study abroad programs have access to library support."

"The 30 programs mentioned in the next question are university-specific; however, our students have access to many more study abroad programs through partnerships with other institutions/organizations."

"The University offers study abroad programs and also has cooperative agreements with a number of international institutions offering our degrees from the host institutions. All are eligible for library support."

"The university sponsors 7 travel-study programs. In addition, students can study at approximately 150 different international institutions through the university system's Education Abroad Program, or at a number of other study abroad programs affiliated with the university through the International Opportunities Program."

If yes, please enter the number of study abroad programs and the number that receive library support. Please enter a whole number. An approximation is acceptable. N=42

Number of study abroad programs N=42

Minimum	Maximum	Mean	Median	Std Dev
2	1200	140.81	50	236.44

Number of programs that receive library support N=38

Minimum	Maximum	Mean	Median	Std Dev
0	1200	87.74	23	202.07

Number of study abroad programs:	Number that receive library support:
2	2
6	6
7	7
7	7
10	10
25	25
30	30
39	39
47	47
50	3
50	50
50	50
50	50
70	70
75	75
85	85
110	110
150	150
160	160
162	162
200	200
200	200

Number of study abroad programs:	Number that receive library support:
275	275
300	300
350	21
1200	1200
2	0
15	0
15	0
25	0
30	0
50	0
51	0
90	0
145	0
260	0
300	0
990	0
7	—
12	—
92	—
120	*

* "The programs don't receive library support but the individual students are supported. All students studying abroad have full access to most online resources. We also, on a case-by-case basis, scan and deliver articles or chapters of books to students abroad."

If the library supports any of the study abroad programs, please complete the survey.

If there are no study abroad programs or they do not receive library support, please submit the survey now.

DESCRIPTION OF STUDY ABROAD PROGRAM

The questions below seek a brief description of the scope of the study abroad program. If your university/institution has multiple programs, please select **one** that receives library support and answer the remaining questions based on that program.

2. At what kind of location is the study abroad program offered? N=30

At a campus administered by a partner host institution	15	50%
At a campus administered by the home institution	3	10%
Other (e.g., semester at sea, rented building, etc.)	12	40%

Please describe other location.

"All of the above." (2 responses)

"Exchange agreements."

"The university offers a wide variety of overseas study opportunities, including direct enrollment at partner institutions abroad, courses for foreigners at host institutions abroad, courses arranged by third party providers in space rented or owned by them, courses offered by our own faculty at locations abroad using space of partner institutions, rented space or field stations."

"Semester at Sea."

"Since 2005, the College of Design's Rome Program has been located in the historic center of the city near the Tiber River in the Palazzo Cenci-Bolognetti at Piazza delle Cinque Scole 23. The College of Design leases 14 rooms on the second floor of the building from the Istituto Pasteur - Fondazione Cenci Bolognetti, a scientific institute affiliated with the Institut Pasteur of Paris and with the University of Rome. In addition, a small area is also leased on the ground floor of the building, which is used primarily for integrated studio arts and model building. (From: College of Design Rome Program Handbook, 2008/2009)."

"The university maintains a facility in Prague and students live in a small hotel located on the outskirts of the city."

"The Summer Session Study Abroad offers a wide range of courses, some of which are taught at a campus administered by a partner institution, while others use rented facilities."

3. Please provide the following details about the program: Location (city and country), subject(s) offered, duration of program (year, semester, summer, independent study, etc.), number of students, number of faculty. N=24

Location:	Subject(s) offered:	Duration of program:	Number of students:	Number of faculty:
Around the world	Anthropology, art history, biology, business, history, music, religious studies, women's studies, etc.	Semester	500–700	25–30
Keio University, Tokyo, Japan	Japanese language, International Studies	Either 1 semester or 1 academic year	N/A	N/A
Brisbane, Australia	Arts, Business, Media Studies, Education, Engineering, Health, Performing Arts, Science, Social Sciences	Term	N/A	N/A
London, UK	Comprehensive university curriculum	Semester	30	2 and 20+ from partner institution
19 locations in 18 countries and 4 continents	Language and Literature, History, Cultural Studies	5 to 8 weeks	325	50
All over the globe	Many subjects covered, too many to name!	All mentioned		
Florence, Italy	Studio Art, Languages, Art History, Women's Studies, Architecture, Social Sciences, Humanities	Semester and Summer	N/A	45
Istanbul, Turkey	Most courses of study are available	Year	6	0
Prague, Czech Republic	Design, English, Foreign Languages, Philosophy, Entomology	Semester, summer, or year	Varies	Rotating faculty and one staff as director
Various	Various	Various	1688 in 2006-07	25
Segovia, Spain	Spanish Language, Literature and Civilization	Summer	35	1
Giessen, Germany	Engineering	Semester	N/A	N/A
Canberra, Australia. Australian National University	Liberal Arts	Semester	N/A	N/A
Siena, Italy	Italian, Political Science, History,	Semester or Year	10	N/A

Location:	Subject(s) offered:	Duration of program:	Number of students:	Number of faculty:
Beijing, China, Cairo, Egypt, multiple cities in Germany, Panama	Arts and Sciences, Humanities, Business, Communications, Computer Sciences, Education, Engineering, Justice Administration and Public Administration	Various length	753	68
Hatfield, England	Comprehensive	Semester or year	Approximately 5 students attend annually	0 US faculty participate
Stellenbosch, South Africa	Public Health, Democracy and Development	1 quarter	30	N/A
Rome, Italy	Architecture, Art and Design, Interior Design, Integrated Studio Arts, Landscape Architecture, Graphic Design, Community and Regional Planning	Full semester or summer options	140 per year	Per year: 10 US faculty, 2 local faculty, plus several local instructors for Italian, Art History, and photography.
Singapore	Communication (B.A.), Business Administration (B.S.), MBA, Executive MBA	Three years, summer	N/A	N/A
Brig, Switzerland	Accounting, Business Ethics, International Law, International Tourism, Finance, Human Resources, Hospitality, French, and German	Fall and Spring Semester Program, with the international portion taking place from October to December in Fall, and January to March in Spring.	Approximately 20 per semester	2–3 faculty per semester
Salzburg, Austria	German language, literature, and culture	Academic quarter	18–20	1
Seville, Spain	Spanish, history, dance	Semester	N/A	N/A
Jerusalem, Israel	Ancient & Modern Near Eastern studies; language (Hebrew & Arabic); Old & New Testament	Three 4-month programs offered on an annual basis	Up to 170	8
Todi, Italy	Art history, Italian, Italian culture	Summer	Approximately 20–25	3

LIBRARY SUPPORT PROVIDED TO STUDY ABROAD PROGRAM

4. How are library services and access to library resources provided to students and faculty in this program? Check all that apply. N=31

Students/faculty have remote access to online resources through the home institution in North America	31	100%
Employees at the home institution in North America provide library services remotely	23	74%
Students/faculty have access to physical collections provided by a partner host institution at the study abroad site	14	45%
Students/faculty have access to online resources through the host institution abroad	12	39%
Employees of the partner host institution provide library services	10	32%
Students/faculty have access to physical collections provided by the home institution at the study abroad site	9	29%
Employees of the home institution provide library services at the study abroad site	5	16%
Other	4	13%

Please describe other method.

"Director of the program checks out books to students, but does not offer in-depth library services."

"Electronic reading materials are provided by the Library depending on the course materials selected by the faculty."

"Most programs are held at universities with full library services and collections."

"Students at the Singapore Institute of Management campus must complete the Library Skills Workbook. The SIM program coordinators developed a version for their use, and also administer instruction and grading for it."

Please enter any additional comments about how library services and access to library resources are provided to students and faculty in this study abroad program below.

"All of the same services that are provided to any student, faculty or staff member not in our buildings. For example: ILL of journal articles or other items that can be delivered/retrieved electronically. Instant messaging, e-mail or telephone reference and research consultations. Access to all electronic resources. Access to Web page guides, tutorials and other information."

"As is the case with all study abroad programs, students and faculty participating in the Rome Program can access all of the online collections and services offered by the e-Library, as long as they have access to the Internet and a Web browser. Remote users—whether they are merely 'off campus' or outside the country— simply use their University ID numbers to authenticate themselves via proxy servers, and thereby gain access to all the content licensed by the Library. Remote users can also make use of Web-based services such as the chat reference service provided by subject librarians. In addition to these services provided by the Library, participants in the Rome Program have access to a small, on-site Library described in the program handbooks as follows: 'The studio facility contains a small library collection that is intended to provide you with basic research materials and information pertaining to your classes and experiences in Rome. The collection is limited and yet provides an invaluable resource to all program participants. Books and other materials may be borrowed if signed out, but you are asked to keep all library materials, with the exception of travel guides, cookbooks and popular fiction titles, in the studio facility at all times to ensure accessibility to the books for all participants.' Participants 'are also encouraged to make use of other public libraries in the city.'"

"Most of our support for international studies is through our ILL/document delivery service. If a student is registered at the university, s/he can request electronic delivery of articles and sections of books from us or through ILL. Semester at Sea is the only program for which we provide a circulating collection."

"Students are provided with a library orientation at the home institution prior to their departure."

"Students: we sent articles electronically through ILL. Faculty/Staff: we send articles electronically through ILL and provide e-document delivery of articles in our collections."

"Study Abroad Students can request both books and articles to be sent to them."

"Students, faculty, and staff with a valid NetID and a 'wireless and library resources' connection have access to all the resources that are available remotely. This is the most common type of access to library resources by students and faculty participating in a study abroad program. In 2006, however, traditional materials were selected by faculty and subject librarians and shipped to Croatia, where the Curator of the Slavic and East European Collection joined the program and provided active support."

"The Library offers virtual lists of library resources for students preparing to study abroad, and for students from abroad coming her."

"We support all study abroad programs equally, thus it is hard to identify one. We assume, but do not know, that our students are given access to library services from the host institution. In addition, our students continue to have access to all online services, including research databases and virtual reference."

5. Which unit administers library support for students and faculty in this study abroad program? Check all that apply. N=31

Home institution Library	30	97%
Host institution Library	11	36%
Home institution Study Abroad Office	6	19%
Home institution Academic Department	3	10%
Home institution Distance Education	2	7%
Other	5	16%

Please describe other unit.

"Director uses a manual check-out system to charge out books to the students."

"Host institution libraries may be providing library services of which we are unaware."

"The College of Design funds and maintains the on-site, studio facility library."

"The home institution develops and supports online resources and the content of the Library Skills Workbook. The host institution administers the Workbook for students at their campus."

"The library provides a range of services as noted previously to all affiliated remote users but not because of their status as a study abroad participant."

6. If the home institution library administers library support for this study abroad program, is there a single individual who has administrative responsibility? N=30

Yes	11	37%
No	19	63%

If yes, please give the following information about that individual: Individual's position title, individual's unit or department, to whom individual reports.

Individual's position title:	Individual's unit or department:	Individual reports to:
Coordinator, Distance Learning Library Services	Distance Learning Library Services, Ekstrom Library	Associate Dean/Director of Ekstrom Library
Director, Design Library	Design Library	Deputy Director of Libraries
Director, Public Services, University Libraries		Associate Vice President for University Libraries
Distance Education Coordinator	Reference & Instruction	Head of Reference
Librarian	University Library	Associate Dean
Manager, Access Services	Access Services	Assistant Dean for Public Services and Outreach
Middle East Studies Librarian	Social Sciences Dept.	Assistant University Librarian for Public Services
Outreach Librarian for Multicultural Services	Office of Services	Scott Walter, Associate University Librarian for Services
Reference Librarian	Reference	Head of Reference
Semester at Sea Librarian	Reference and Information Services	Head, Reference and Information Services
International Program Support Librarian		Associate University Librarian for Collections and International Programs

If a single individual does not have this administrative responsibility, please describe how library support for this study abroad program is administered. N=13

"Electronic access to library resources and library services is provided by several departments on the campus, including the Libraries and University Information Technology Services."

"Same as all off-campus services: online."

"Services to all students at a distance are built into existing services: ILL, e-reference, and access to online resources."

"Services to remote users, access to electronic resources etc. are administered across and throughout the library."

"Study Abroad students are treated exactly like our other distance education students. They can obtain reference assistance and instruction via e-mail, chat, and phone. These services are provided by the Reference Department. Study abroad students also can request delivery of books via snail mail and articles or chapters via email (scanned copies). They can also make ILL requests, although we do not send other libraries physical books overseas. We fill ILL requests for Study Abroad students only if they can be filled electronically. All of these services—ILL, book delivery, scanning—are provided by our ILL Department."

"The authentication of university affiliation is done by issuing a valid university card."

"The Director of Public Services is the primary library contact for the program, and often refers specific requests for assistance or services to others at the home institution."

"The Distance Education librarian position at Gelman is relatively new and is mainly supported by GW graduate distance/online programs. No formal agreement is yet in place with the Studies Abroad Programs; however, we do fulfill requests (and have done so in the past) for resources from students in programs abroad as part of our regular services."

"The Library's Associate Dean for Research & Access is responsible, broadly speaking, for all access services for all user groups. The latter includes remote users in general, and study abroad participants in particular. On-site in Rome, the College of Design employs a Resident Director, whose responsibilities include oversight of the studio facility library."

"The on-site librarian and support staff are not library employees. However, requests for materials are handled by home library staff."

"University faculty directly utilize the services for all electronic forms of support provided by the university. Additionally, online materials are available to the students. All materials assigned can be accessed by students from abroad. These are materials in addition to the host/partner university's library."

"Via all library departments—as if students and faculty were on campus."

"While I am the point person for this program, students and faculty do not need to go through me to get library service and resources. Our Interlibrary Loan Office supports requests for materials that can be delivered electronically. Our Circulation Department makes sure students and faculty are in the Library Patron Database, so they may continue to access the library's electronic resources while abroad. Our subject specialists provide consultations for students with specific research needs, and our general reference services support questions through e-mail and chat."

FUNDING OF LIBRARY SUPPORT FOR STUDY ABROAD PROGRAM

7. How is library support for this study abroad program funded? Check all that apply. N=31

Home institution's library general budget	19	61%
Home institution's library acquisitions budget	14	45%
Home institution's library personnel budget	9	29%
Home institution's general budget	8	26%
Host institution's budget	6	19%
Student fees	4	13%
Home institution's separate budget for study abroad program	2	7%
Endowment funding	1	3%
Gifts	1	3%
Other	6	19%

Please describe other source of funding.

"Because there are no special services provided to faculty and students in the Rome Program (or other study abroad programs), there is no separate budget within the Library to support these programs. Funding for the e-Library's online collections and services comes from the Library's general budget (Materials and Access budget for online collections; Operating Budget for salaries, supplies, and services.) Costs associated with the small, studio facility library in Rome are borne by the College of Design."

"Designated portion of tuition allocated to library."

"Funded through program administrator."

"Host institution provides print resources and some digital resources. All host institution students have full access to home institution online resources."

"No additional funding."

"This work is absorbed into regular collections and services."

STUDY ABROAD PROGRAM LIBRARY

If employees of the home institution provide library services and access to library resources in a physical location at the study abroad site, please answer the following questions about the collections, equipment, and staff in that facility.

If not, please Click here to skip the questions about the physical location and continue to the next set of questions.

Study Abroad Program Library: Collections

8. Please indicate the size of the physical collection, if this data is readily available. N=4

Monographic volumes:	Serial titles:	Audio items:	Cartographic materials:	Films and videos:	Microform units:	Other material:
104	5					
1000						Other materials include a small number of journals, course readers, guides, dictionaries, maps, exhibition catalogues, DVDs, and VCR tapes.
5584	20	50		250		
8000	0	40	70	900	0	

9. If an exact count of material is not readily available, please provide a general description of the size of the collection. N=1

"12,000 items in library. A media lab includes a slide library as well as a digital image database for personal image collections of faculty and staff (the Visual Resource Collaborative)."

10. Are these materials catalogued? N=5

Yes	5	100%
No	0	—

Comments

"Items can be located by author, title, or broad category on an Excel spreadsheet."

"Monographs cataloged into LC call numbers. Serials are alphabetic. Audio, Videos & DVDs are given accession numbers."

11. Are materials included and searchable in the home institution's OPAC? N=5

Yes	2	40%
No	3	60%

Comment

"Records are stored on the home institution catalog but are 'shadowed' from public view. They are searchable by the public only from on board the ship."

12. Are these materials searchable as a discrete collection? N=5

Yes	5	100%
No	0	—

Comments

"See preceding comments. 'Searchable' within the context of an online Excel spreadsheet."

"They are searchable by the public on shipboard but not from the home OPAC."

13. Do materials in this collection circulate? N=5

	Yes	No
Monographs	5	—
Periodicals	2	3
Audio/Visual material	4	—
Other category of material	1	1

If yes, what is the loan period?

Monographs	Periodicals	Audio/visuals	Other materials	Students:	Faculty:	Staff:
Yes	No	Yes		2 weeks	2 weeks	2 weeks
Yes	Yes	Yes	Yes	Indefinite, until requested by another user.	Indefinite, until requested by another user.	Indefinite, until requested by another user.
Yes	Yes			Varies	Varies	Varies
Yes	No	Yes				
Yes	No	Yes	No	2 weeks for general collection on shipboard only	2 weeks for general collection on shipboard only	2 weeks for general collection on shipboard only

Study Abroad Program Library: Equipment and Staffing

14. What equipment is available for use by study abroad students and faculty in this facility? Check all that apply. N=5

Desktop computers	5	100%
Printers	5	100%
Photocopiers	4	80%
Scanners	2	40%
Video equipment	2	40%
Loaner laptop computers	1	20%
Other	3	60%

Please describe other equipment.

"Wireless Internet connection; the library does not supply any of the equipment."

"Wireless Internet access is provided."

"99% of students bring their own laptop computers on the program. However, the studio facility/library also provides the following equipment: two desktop PCs; three desktop MACs; one HP1300n laser printer; one networked Konica color printer/copier, A3&A4 size; two scanners; two LCD projectors; one video camera; and one Canon digital camera."

15. For each category of staff below please indicate how many individuals work in this facility (enter a whole number, e.g., 4) and the FTE of these individuals (enter a whole number or a two-digit decimal, e.g., 3.25). Also enter the total number of staff in the facility in all categories and their total FTE. N=5

	1	2	3	4	5
Librarian, individuals	2	1			
Librarian, FTE	2	—			
Other professional, individuals			1	1	1
Other professional, FTE			1	1	0.25
Support staff, individuals		2			
Support staff, FTE		—			
Student assistants, individuals	4–4				
Student assistants, FTE	1–1.5				
Total number of individuals	6–8	3	1	1	1
Total FTE	3–3.5	—	1	1	0.25

Please describe the "Other professional" staff category.

"The individual here that manages the library is actually the office manager for the Jerusalem Center."

"Resident Director."

"On-site director of the program; she devotes a small percentage of her time (ca. 1%) to library-related duties."

ONLINE LIBRARY RESOURCES FOR THE STUDY ABROAD PROGRAM

16. Who may access online resources provided by the home institution? Check all that apply. N=33

Any currently enrolled student with a valid ID/computer account

may access online resources from anywhere they have Internet access   33   100%

Any currently employed faculty member with a valid ID/computer

account may access online resources from anywhere they have Internet access   32   97%

Any currently employed staff member with a valid ID/computer

 account may access online resources from anywhere they have Internet access   30   91%

Other   1   3%

Please describe other.

"Postdoctoral fellows with valid ID/login may access online resources from anywhere they have Internet access."

17. **Do study abroad students and faculty have access to the same online resources and services as those at the home institution? N=33**

Yes	31	94%
No	2	6%

If no, please explain the differences.

"They have access to the same online resources but some services are only available locally from the home institution."

"There are a handful of databases that require a user to be located on campus and thus are not available to students abroad."

LIBRARY SERVICES FOR THE STUDY ABROAD PROGRAM

18. **What library services are offered to students and faculty in this study abroad program? Check all that apply. N=30**

Reference	29	94%
Document delivery	21	68%
Interlibrary Loan	16	52%
Library instruction	11	36%
Other, please describe	8	26%

Reference	Document Delivery	Interlibrary Loan	Library Instruction	Other, please describe
✓	✓	✓	✓	
✓	✓	✓	✓	
✓	✓	✓	✓	
✓	✓	✓	✓	Library instruction that is available online. ILL of items that can be delivered electronically. Document Delivery of photocopies or scans of articles from the Libraries' hard-copy subscriptions for a fee.
✓	✓	✓	✓	
✓	✓	✓	✓	The only service we do not provide for Study Abroad students is mailing other universities' books to them as ILLs. We do, however, mail books from our own collections.
✓	✓	✓	✓	
✓	✓	✓	✓	
✓	✓	✓		At various times, we have made course readings and other instructional support materials available to study abroad participants (including students in the College of Design Rome Program) through two different library services: e-Reserve, and the Instruction Commons. The former is simply the electronic version of our traditional course reserve service, and focuses primarily on digitized versions of journal articles, book chapters, etc. The Instruction Commons, according to the program Web site, is "a collaborative Web-based library instruction program. Class instructors and subject-specialist librarians collaborate together to compile library research tools and other information sources that are relevant to specific class assignments and learning objectives, and to make these resources easily accessible to students through the Commons Web site, along with other class materials." The Library is in the process of combining these two programs into a single Course Reserves & Resources service.
✓	✓	✓		Although we do not offer library instruction classes specifically for students entering our study abroad programs, we do have a number of guides linked from our Web page, a distance education blog, and numerous online tutorials available.

Reference	Document Delivery	Interlibrary Loan	Library Instruction	Other, please describe
✓	✓	✓		
✓	✓	✓		
✓	✓	✓		
✓	✓	✓		Online document delivery
✓	✓	✓		Pre-departure orientation (library-related). Interlibrary Loan and Document delivery are limited to electronic materials.
✓	✓			Any online electronic materials
✓	✓			
✓	✓			
✓	✓		✓	
✓	✓		✓	
✓		✓	✓	Virtual Resources. Also, all students at the University, including Study Abroad Students, may use the reference, ILL and instruction services provided through the University Library System.
✓			✓	
✓				
✓				
✓				
✓				
✓				
✓				
✓				
	✓			

19. Please indicate how the library services below are delivered to students and faculty in this study abroad program. Check all that apply. N=28

Reference	By onsite library staff	By library staff at the home institution	By library staff at the host institution	N
E-mail	3	26	3	27
Chat/instant messaging	2	22	1	24
Phone	2	18	3	20
Mail	2	14	3	15
Face-to-face	4	3	8	13
VoIP	1	2	1	4
Other	—	2	—	2

Please describe other delivery method.

"Chat reference service offered by home institution is generally not open when classes are in session at the host institution (12 hour time difference), so most reference takes place at the host institution."

"For the 'by library staff at the host institution' column: We really do not know the answer to what the host offers. Our assumption is that full library services are generally available."

"Research guides."

"The Web site is linked from the Library and Study Abroad Web sites."

"We are currently developing a Web page that lists and describes Library resources and services targeted specifically to Summer Session Study Abroad participants."

Instruction	By onsite library staff	By library staff at the home institution	By library staff at the host institution	N
E-mail	1	10	3	13
Chat/instant messaging	1	10	1	11
Phone	1	7	3	10
Face-to-face	2	2	6	9
Mail	1	4	2	6
VoIP	—	1	—	1
Other	—	4	1	4

Please describe other delivery method.

"As previously mentioned, the Library Skills Workbook graduation requirement for undergraduates is a shared effort."

"Online tutorials."

"Online tutorials, distance education blog, and 'Services for Off-Campus Patrons' Web page with links to several guides directed at anyone who needs remote access to our collections and services."

"The Web site has online tutorials for using the libraries' catalog and certain databases. Individual instruction is delivered in the same ways reference is delivered."

20. **Is the library using any pre-recorded/pre-produced instruction modules, such as Camtasia or Libguides, to deliver instruction to these study abroad students or faculty? N=30**

Yes	11	37%
No	19	63%

If yes, please describe what kind of software is being used and for what purposes.

"60-second tutorials created using Camtasia. Also using Libquides, but more for discipline specific materials than for modules."

"CamStudio was used to create a screencast for orienting distance students to the Libraries' resources and services. A pilot project is in place to create more screencasts for this purpose."

"Camtasia, YouTube for online tutorials."

"Dedicated Web-based resource guides."

"Searchpath for basic library instruction is available via the library Web site."

"The home institution has developed instruction modules through Camtasia and are available to the students at the Jerusalem Center."

"There are a series of Study Abroad tutorials that have been produced by the library. HTML/CSS was used to create these. We also have some produced some Web pages for specific programs (such as the Transatlantic Masters Program)."

"We are using Captivate for our tutorials. Tutorials cover basic topics such as learning to use the catalog and how to look for a journal article. None of the tutorials are aimed solely at the study abroad audience, however."

"We have just started migrating our existing research guides to the Libguides platform and we have developed a series of online tutorials (Dreamweaver/Captivate) to teach users how to access and use resources."

"We offer a series of online tutorials (produced in-house)."

21. Is the library using any social software, such as blogs, wikis, Facebook, or Second Life, to deliver services to study abroad students or faculty? N=31

Yes	8	26%
No	23	74%

If yes, please describe what kind of software is being used and for what purposes.

"As mentioned above, we have a distance education blog. We also have a number of blogs and wikis that are subject oriented, rather than oriented specifically to the study abroad audience. And we have a Facebook page. We use Wikimedia for the wikis and WordPress for the blogs."

"blogs, wikis."

"Students can use chat software to 'chat' with librarians in real time."

"Study abroad students would have access to the same Internet delivered services (Wikis and Facebook) as local students, however these services are not expressly designed or marketed to study abroad students."

"The Libraries have a Facebook page and the librarians who monitor it note that many international students—some enrolled and some prospective students—use it extensively. There is also a 'Services for Students' blog which feeds to the page and is available thru RSS."

"We are using blogs and wikis in overall instructional efforts. Students at a distance may be participating, although the blogs/wikis are not specifically for this group of students."

"We do use blogs/wikis/Facebook but have not specifically targeted them to this population."

"We use social software as noted above but it is intended for all students not just study abroad students."

LIBRARY SERVICES FOR THE STUDY ABROAD PROGRAM, CONT.

22. What kind of interlibrary loan and/or document delivery services does the home institution library offer to these study abroad students and faculty? Check all that apply. N=28

The home institution library delivers electronic materials directly to study abroad students and faculty	26	93%
The home institution library delivers hard copy materials directly to study abroad students and faculty	14	50%
The home institution library delivers electronic materials to the study abroad library	3	11%

The home institution library delivers hard copy

materials to the study abroad library   1   4%

Additional comments about interlibrary loan/document delivery:

"Faculty at the home institution may check out materials at home and keep them for a semester for use at the study abroad site."

"Hard copy materials from the Libraries only are delivered by mail to study abroad students; no interlibrary loan is provided for hard copy materials."

"Not sure if anyone has ever requested that we deliver hard copy materials directly to study abroad students or faculty, but we would do so if necessary."

"The host institution has a very strong onsite collection and excellent services, so students rarely use the services of the home institution for these needs."

"These services are available to all students enrolled at the University, including Study Abroad students."

"To obtain a 'returnable' item (e.g., the hard copy of a book) from the Library, a study abroad participant would need to request the item via the Library's Document Delivery Service, and pay the associated fees. The same would be true if the individual wanted to obtain a copy of an article in a journal that was held by the Library, but that was not available electronically. Study abroad participants can also use the Library's Interlibrary Loan service to request non-returnable items—primarily journal articles—from other libraries, at no charge."

"We scan and deliver articles and chapters of books to students abroad on a case-by-case basis."

CHALLENGES OF LIBRARY SUPPORT FOR STUDY ABROAD PROGRAMS

23. Please describe up to three of the biggest challenges in providing library support to study abroad participants. N=24

Challenge 1	Challenge 2	Challenge 3
Access to Online Resources: Although students and faculty should have access to all electronic resources available through the library's proxied remote access service, there are occasional access problems that may be due to Internet infrastructure at the abroad site.	Acquisitions: Materials ordered by the home institution are shipped directly to the study abroad location. It can be difficult to verify receipt of materials for which we are invoiced.	

Challenge 1	Challenge 2	Challenge 3
Appreciation by the student of the need to prepare in advance for remote authentication to library digital resources.	Ditto	Ditto
At locations where students are not affiliated with a local academic institution abroad they generally rely on small reference collections. Therefore they must rely more heavily on the home campus electronic library resources.	Some students, particularly those studying in the developing world, have difficulty in accessing home campus electronic library resources due to limited availability of Internet access, poor Internet connections, limited bandwidth, and power outages.	
Awareness. We suspect that many Study Abroad students are unaware that they are eligible to continue receiving full library services while they are away.		
Costs and security of delivering hard copy library materials.	Institutional/policy constraints to providing document delivery to students.	Communication and familiarity with the large number of host institution libraries.
Delays due to time zones, requests come from international sites during the night so responses to students are delayed until next morning	Providing instruction, guidelines, Web sites in other languages	Students in remote locations cannot have face-to-face assistance, all communication is via the Internet or phone, often requesters cannot browse the collections.
Getting materials to Prague if we buy them here. Typically, we order materials in the Czech Republic from a bookstore there and catalog them based on order records. Barcodes and labels are then sent to Prague for the Director to affix to the materials.		
Getting the word out to all students that library services and resources are available to them regardless of where they are.	We generally don't have the budget to deliver hard copy materials to students abroad.	We have a large number of study abroad programs in many countries. We would like to create tailor-made resources for each, and perhaps we will get there, but it requires many resources (mainly people and time).

Challenge 1	Challenge 2	Challenge 3
Knowing whether onsite professors require students to use library materials for classes.	Providing library use instruction to faculty and students other than the modules available online.	Lack of qualified people onsite to assist library patrons.
Lack of awareness by study abroad participants that we provide these services.	Communicating with study abroad participants.	Distance.
Lack of opportunities to explain full range of library services available to students abroad	Reliability of ISP services in participants' study abroad country	Time differential in providing reference services such as IM/Chat which is not provided at the home institution on a 24/7 basis.
Limited services for distance students. Service level is not the same as for on campus students.	Need for building relationships with and ongoing communication with Study Abroad office.	Funding!
No special services are provided—study abroad students have same access as any student from a remote site.		
Not enough funding	Changes in leadership for the various study abroad programs	
One challenge involved inciting support from the Study Abroad Office to collaborate. So, I created the online resources, which are linked from the Library. Once the resource page was completed, the Study Abroad Office was much more willing to collaborate.	I wanted to offer an instruction session to students preparing to study abroad and also for students from abroad coming to Illinois. The office however indicated that the orientation schedule for their programs were already full. As a result, we are discussing methods to promote the virtual resources and also translating the Web resources into print handouts.	
One of the biggest challenges is getting the attention of students before they leave our campus. They're both excited and worried about the prospect of living in another country, and their minds tend to be on anything and everything but library resources and services.	Another challenge is just how to make it easier for these students to find the information they need, no matter where they are — though we have that constant challenge with on-campus users as well.	It's difficult to keep up with the ever-increasing number and variety of study abroad opportunities on this campus, therefore difficult to know how well we're meeting needs.
Reliability of access in some countries		

Challenge 1	Challenge 2	Challenge 3
Small physical space of the shipboard library.	Library is open 24/7, but not staffed 24/7.	Slow delivery of electronic resources due to limited internet bandwidth on shipboard.
Technical problems related to access to online resources.	Time differences.	Major growth plans for students enrolled in partner institution programs have budgetary implications for online resource subscriptions.
The fact that programs are not offered at a facility administered by the home institution limits the range of resources and services that can be provided.	Creating student and faculty awareness of the range of resources and services that are available to them is much more difficult and energy-consuming than actually making those resources available.	Engaging faculty in a serious cooperative effort geared towards the selection and provision of library resources.
Time differences between Europe and America	The library does not offer instruction to students before they go abroad so that the students might face an "information emergency" without awareness of what the library can do for them.	Cost of delivering items can be prohibitive and the time it takes for delivery can cause issues.
We currently have no formal relation/agreement with the Studies Abroad Programs Office, which means that neither program administrators nor faculty may be familiar with our services.	Physical delivery of books has obvious limitations because of time constraints.	Censorship in some of the host countries has restricted access to online materials.
While it is relatively easy for study abroad participants to have Web-based access to a wealth of e-journal literature and a growing number of e-books, it is still awkward, time-consuming, and probably not cost effective to try to ship hard-copy books internationally. Fortunately, the demand for the latter seems almost non-existent.	While we assert that study abroad participants have the same access to e-library collections and services that our local users enjoy (as long as they authenticate via a proxy server), the reality may be that hardware, software, and network/bandwidth issues abroad may severely limit that access, or make it impracticable.	

CHANGES OVER TIME

24. In the last five years has the number of study abroad programs at your university/institution Increased, Decreased, or Stayed about the same? N=28

25. In the last five years has the number of study abroad programs that receive library support Increased, Decreased, or Stayed about the same? N=29

26. In the coming five years is it anticipated that the number of study abroad programs at your university/institution will Increase, Decrease, or Stay about the same? N=28

27. In the coming five years is it anticipated that the number of study abroad programs that receive library support will Increase, Decrease, or Stay about the same? N=28

Number of programs have:	Programs that receive library support have:	Number of programs will:	Programs that receive library support will:
Decreased	Decreased	Stay about the same	Stay about the same
Increased	Stayed about the same	Stay about the same	Increase
Increased	Stayed about the same	Increase	Increase
Increased	Stayed about the same	Increase	Stay about the same
Increased	Increased	Increase	Increase
Increased	Increased	Stay about the same	Stay about the same
Increased	Stayed about the same	Increase	Stay about the same
Increased	Increased	Increase	Increase
Increased	Increased	Increase	Increase
Increased	Increased	Increase	Increase
Increased	Increased	Increase	Increase
Increased	Increased	Increase	Increase
Increased	Increased	Increase	Increase
Increased	Increased	Increase	Increase
Increased	Increased	Increase	Increase
Increased	Stayed about the same	Increase	Stay about the same
Increased	Stayed about the same	Increase	Stay about the same
Increased	Increased	Increase	Increase
Increased	Increased	Increase	Increase

Number of programs have:	Programs that receive library support have:	Number of programs will:	Programs that receive library support will:
Stayed about the same	Stayed about the same	Stay about the same	Stay about the same
Stayed about the same	Stayed about the same	Stay about the same	Stay about the same
Stayed about the same	Stayed about the same	Stay about the same	Stay about the same
Stayed about the same	Stayed about the same	Decrease	Decrease
Stayed about the same	Stayed about the same	Stay about the same	Stay about the same
Stayed about the same	Stayed about the same	—	—
Stayed about the same	Stayed about the same	Stay about the same	Stay about the same
—	Increased	Increase	Increase

ADDITIONAL COMMENTS

28. Please enter any additional information about library support for study abroad programs that may assist the author in accurately analyzing the results of this survey. N=9

"In the fall of 2007 the Library surveyed ca. 400 students who had spent the summer abroad. The survey focused on students' library and information needs and how and to what extent they are met. Based on the survey results, we are developing a pre-departure orientation focused on library and information resources, to be followed by another return survey."

"Most services to study abroad participants are available to all members of the University community. Remote patron services in general are developed with study abroad participants in mind. Education and outreach to study abroad participants is the primary component of library service to this group."

"Subject librarians were very involved in the startup of this program, and provided consultation on specific titles for the host institution to purchase to support the programs. We also had an onsite visit by the host institution program administrator and librarian to learn more about our services and collections. Librarians from home plan to visit SIM in the future."

"We do not have any particular initiatives aimed at study abroad participants. We have a large number of distance students (remote users) to begin with and we provide the same level of support for study abroad students as we do for distance students. At this point we are not sure that the students heading off to study abroad programs know that the services we have for distance users apply to them. Anecdotally, we do get feedback every semester from students who go abroad and tell us that their access to our library's databases and full-text journals were a lifesaver."

"We probably need to examine our marketing to make sure study abroad students know what resources and services are available to them remotely, especially for all of the other study abroad options offered by the university."

RESPONDING INSTITUTIONS

University at Albany, SUNY

University of Alberta

University of Arizona

Boston College

Brigham Young University

University of British Columbia

University at Buffalo, SUNY

University of California, Irvine

University of California, San Diego

University of California, Santa Barbara

Canada Institute for Scientific and Technical Information

University of Chicago

George Washington University

Georgetown University

University of Georgia

University of Hawaii at Manoa

University of Illinois at Urbana-Champaign

Indiana University Bloomington

University of Iowa

Iowa State University

Kent State University

University of Kentucky

Library of Congress

University of Louisville

University of Manitoba

University of Massachusetts, Amherst

Michigan State University

University of Minnesota

Université de Montréal

University of Nebraska–Lincoln

University of New Mexico

University of North Carolina at Chapel Hill

North Carolina State University

Northwestern University

Ohio University

University of Oklahoma

Oklahoma State University

University of Pennsylvania

Pennsylvania State University

Purdue University

Rice University

Rutgers University

University of Southern California

Southern Illinois University Carbondale

Syracuse University

University of Texas at Austin

Texas Tech University

Vanderbilt University

University of Virginia

Washington State University

Washington University in St. Louis

University of Western Ontario

Yale University

REPRESENTATIVE DOCUMENTS

Study Abroad Program Web Pages

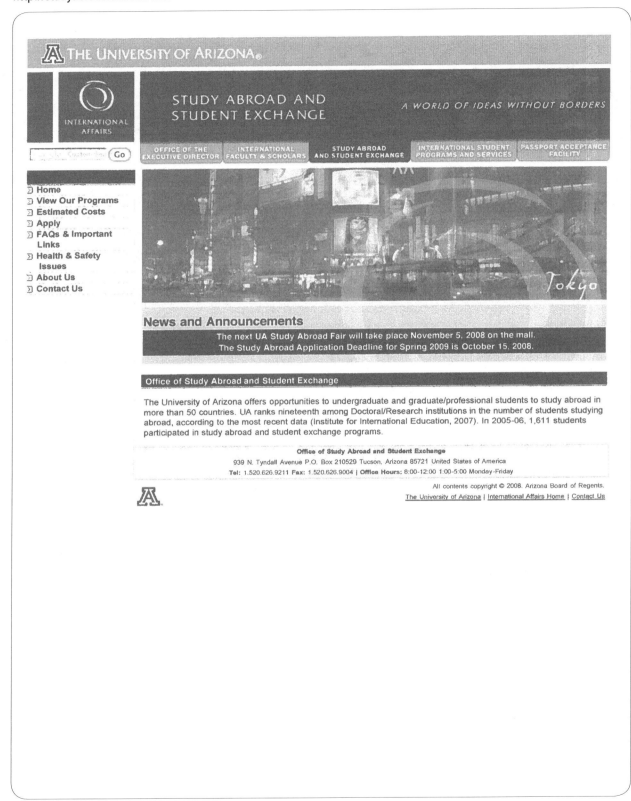

Brigham Young University
JERUSALEM CENTER
for Near Eastern Studies

BYU Jerusalem Center

Beginning in 2009, the BYU Jerusalem Center will eliminate the short 2-month programs and offer three 4-month programs on an annual basis. Program dates and application time-periods are outlined in the general information.

For the present, eligibility is limited to students enrolled at BYU, BYU-Idaho, or BYU-Hawaii.

What is the BYU Jerusalem Center?

The Jerusalem Center is Brigham Young University's center for study in Jerusalem. Students enroll through the BYU campus in Provo, Utah, travel to the Holy Land, and live in the Center for programs that extend for four months. Students study a core curriculum that focuses on Old and New Testament, ancient and modern Near Eastern studies, and language (Hebrew and Arabic). Classroom study is built around field trips that cover the length and breadth of the Holy Land.

The Center itself is a beautiful building on Mount Scopus overlooking the Mount of Olives, the Kidron Valley, and the Old City. The 125,000 square-foot, eight-level structure is set amid five acres of beautifully landscaped gardens. The first five levels (moving up from the lowest level) provide dormitory and apartment space for up to 170 students. Dormitory rooms accommodate four people with ample study space and a private bath. Each of these rooms has a patio overlooking the Old City. The sixth level houses a cafeteria, classrooms, computer facilities, and a gymnasium. Administrative and faculty offices are located on the seventh level, as is a 250-seat auditorium. The main entry is on the eighth level, which also contains a spectacular recital and special events auditorium with organ, lecture rooms, general and reserve libraries, offices, a domed theater, and a learning resource area.

Are the BYU Jerusalem Center facilities open to the public?

The facilities at the Jerusalem Center are available only to full-time students formally enrolled in a BYU Jerusalem Center program. For those interested in visiting the building, a 45-60 minute tour is available. The tour includes a hosting video, a ten-minute organ recital, and a tour of the eighth floor and the Jerusalem Center gardens. To schedule a tour or to obtain information on tour availability, please contact the hosting staff at the Jerusalem Center by calling 011-972-2-626-5666.

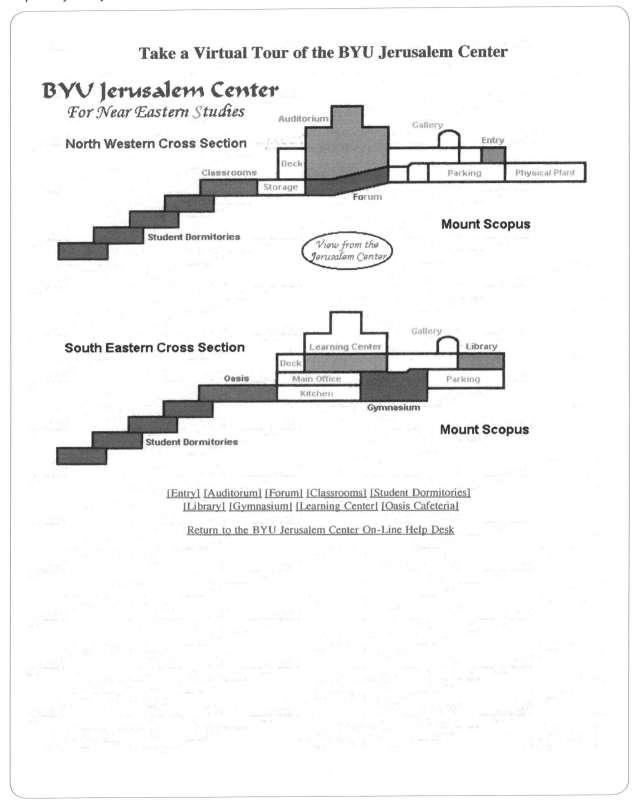

BRIGHAM YOUNG UNIVERSITY: Learning Center

http://ce.byu.edu/jc/tour/learn.htm

Learning Center

The learning center is a beautiful, large, open room with dark blue carpeting set against limestone pillars and arches that divide the room into 12 connected spaces. The learning center is used for special events and can accommodate all students and staff for special dinners and gatherings. A smaller anteroom provides space for receptions and hosting visiting officals. A balcony, the highest at the Center, provides the best view of the old and new Jerusalem.

Return to the BYU Jerusalem Center Virtual Tour Map
Return to the BYU Jerusalem Center On-Line Help Desk

UNIVERSITY OF CALIFORNIA, IRVINE: Center for International Education

http://www.cie.uci.edu/index.shtml

CIE Home : Prospective Participants : Participants : Returnees : Reciprocity Students : Faculty : Contacts : The World at UCI : FAQ

START HERE!

Want to go abroad?
★ START HERE ★

Mission Statement

eGiving

🧳 **DON'T SETTLE**
UCI Center for International Education

NEWS

Applications to study abroad on EAP in spring quarter, summer, or fall 2009 or year 2009-10 will be available starting Welcome Week 2008!

Experience abroad enhances your resume! Watch this tip from the UCI Career Center on YouTube.

How to Study Abroad, Get Out of Irvine, and Travel Away! Read this New University article.

International Education Week 2007 Recap!

GO ABROAD Fair wrap-up and raffle winners! Read what the *New University* had to say about the fair.

CALENDAR

Extended EAP Deadlines

Rolling Deadlines until full:

Germany BEST spring; Hong Kong spring; Hungary spring; Korea spring; Singapore spring; Taiwan spring; Thailand spring.

MORE EAP Deadlines

Information Sessions

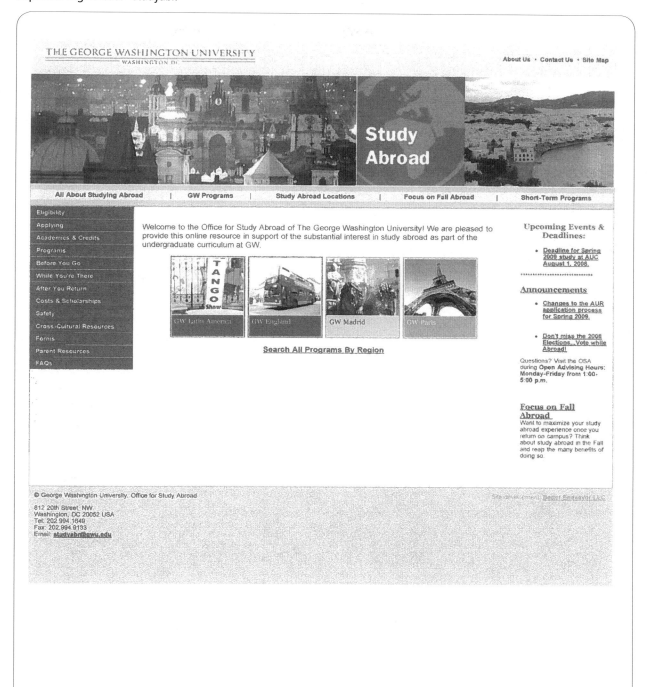

GEORGE WASHINGTON UNIVERSITY: All About Studying Abroad

http://www.studyabroad.gwu.edu/AllAboutStudyingAbroad/index.cfm

HOME · About Us · Contact Us · Site Map

All About Studying Abroad | GW Programs | Study Abroad Locations | Focus on Fall Abroad | Short-Term Programs

Eligibility
Applying
Academics & Credits
Programs
Before You Go
While You're There
After You Return
Costs & Scholarships
Safety
Cross-Cultural Resources
Forms
Parent Resources
FAQs

>> HOME

All About Studying Abroad

In support of the University's mission to "promote the process of lifelong learning from both global and integrative perspectives," the Office for Study Abroad offers international education opportunities through the University's overseas study centers, international exchange partners, and affiliated organizations. As an extension of the University's academic program, GW's study abroad programs provide access to high quality international education programs in expanding geographic destinations to serve a diverse student population representing a wide array of academic disciplines. As educators, we facilitate the academic, personal, professional, and intercultural development of students through the programs and services we provide.

Join Student Listserv

The Office for Study Abroad maintains a listserv for all students and alumni of the study abroad program. We send out important information concerning meeting schedules, announcements, program representative visits, and special events. Generally, one to five messages per week are sent on the listserv, so it will not be a burden to your email account. **Join the listserv now!**

812 20th Street, NW
Washington, DC 20052 USA
Tel: 202.994.1649
Fax: 202.994.9133
Email: **studyabr@gwu.edu**

OFFICE OF INTERNATIONAL PROGRAMS

The mission of the Office of International Programs (OIP) at Georgetown University is to foster the international character of the University by promoting, supporting, and developing a wide range of international and intercultural educational opportunities for members of the Georgetown community.

The Office is divided into two divisions. The Division of International Student and Scholar Services (IS) supports international students and scholars in deriving the maximum advantage from their educational and research experiences at Georgetown. The Division of Overseas Studies (OS) develops and administers international educational opportunities overseas for GU students. The Executive Director of International Programs, Katherine S. Bellows, oversees both divisions.

In coordinating these, and other international projects, the Office of International Programs seeks to foster a sense of community that builds on the universalism of the University's intellectual tradition, and encourages many voices to be heard. OIP facilitates these cross-cultural discussions by sponsoring exchanges of students and faculty and serving as a resource for departments and schools on campus that undertake international and intercultural initiatives.

INTERNATIONAL STUDENT & SCHOLAR SERVICES

OVERSEAS STUDIES

ABOUT OIP

Search | Site Index | Directory | About

1421 37th St. N.W. | 2nd Floor Poulton Hall (above the UPS store) | Box 571013 | Washington, D.C. 20057 | Tel: 202.687.5867 | Fax: 202.687.5944

Home
Programs
Staff

Search | Site Index | Site Map | Directory | About

Login

▸ **Prospective Students**
▸ **Once Nominated**
▸ **While Abroad**
▸ **Back to GU**
Returnee Corner
▸ **Parents**
▸ **Financial Aid & Scholarships**
▸ **Health & Safety**
▸ **Important Dates**
Travel Blog

Welcome to the Division of Overseas Studies website where you will find information about study abroad programs in countries throughout the world.

The mission of Overseas Studies at Georgetown University is to promote, support, and develop international and intercultural educational opportunities for students, and in so doing, help to define the international character of Georgetown. These programs are developed and evaluated in collaboration with the wider Georgetown community to ensure that they are academically rigorous, linguistically appropriate, and complementary to the Georgetown curriculum. In keeping with the Jesuit philosophy of education and service, these overseas opportunities invite participants to reflect on the values that form their own identities, and encourage them to assume their roles as responsible world citizens.

The Office of International Programs offers more than 120 programs in 39 countries. We welcome you to visit our office, discuss your interests, and discover the possibilities of study abroad.

If you experience any technical difficulties, please click here.

Announcements

Resource Center
Summer Hours: Mon-Fri
1:00 pm-4:00 pm

No announcements?
Upgrade Flash or
Text-only

Georgetown University - Office of International Programs - Division of Overseas Studies
Poulton Hall, 2nd Floor - 1421 37th Street NW - Box 571013 - Washington, DC 20057-1013
202-687-5867 (tel) - 202-687-5944 (fax) - overseasstudies@georgetown.edu

Last modified 11/19/2007 Top of page

Georgetown University

Search | Site Index | Site Map | Directory | About

**The University of Hawai'i at Manoa
Study Abroad Center**

*Study, Live
Experience*

Earn University of Hawai'i at Manoa credits for
coursework taken abroad. All students meeting the
program admissions requirements are eligible to
apply. Courses are offered in a wide range of
study in countries throughout the world and can
be used to fulfill your major, language, graduation
or elective requirements.

**PROGRAMS
CALENDAR
APPLICATIONS
FUNDING SOURCES
RESOURCES
ABOUT STUDY ABROAD
CONTACT US**

SAC office hours:
Monday – Friday, 9:00 am – 3:00 pm

Study Abroad Fees and Program Costs

Home | Calendar | Programs | Applications | Funding Sources | Resources | Alumni | Contact Us

Copyright © 1998–2008 University of Hawai'i at Manoa Study Abroad Center
v.2 Design by Pipeline Graphics

https://www.studyabroad.uiuc.edu/

Study Abroad
UNIVERSITY OF ILLINOIS AT URBANA-CHAMPAIGN

home | programs | staff | deadlines

Login

Study Abroad
▸ INFORMATION FOR
▸ IMPORTANT ISSUES
▸ HEALTH & SAFETY
▸ GENERAL LINKS
▸ ABOUT US

Announcements

Office Hours
Study Abroad Office
[View Details]

No announcements?
Upgrade Flash
or View without Flash

search uiuc.edu
(go) search options

Welcome to Study Abroad at the University of Illinois at Urbana-Champaign

"Study Abroad was the best academic and personal choice I have made in college. I learned more about Spain, America and myself than I could have imagined, and in the process improved my Spanish conversation skills and confidence 10-fold." ~ Megan O'Connell: Granada, Spain Sum 06.

"Study Abroad was a turning point in my life. It was the best thing I have done thus far. I saw amazing things and met great people from all over the world. Along with this I learned a great deal about myself and the people in the world." ~ Spencer Masterson: Christchurch, New Zealand, Fall 06.

With *over 350 study abroad* opportunities, the University of Illinois at Urbana-Champaign offers a program to fit your needs! Our programs vary in terms of...

Academic Offerings
Earn credit for your major or minor or try something new! Undergraduate and graduate students can explore their field from an international perspective or step out of their major and take classes in another area of interest. Some programs also offer options for volunteering, internships, or conducting research.

Location
We offer study abroad programs in nearly 60 countries and on every continent except for one--Antarctica!

Length
Students can go abroad for a year, semester, summer, and winter or spring break.

Price
Programs vary considerably in cost. Some are comparable to studying at Illinois, while others can be more expensive. Scholarships are available and financial aid can be applied towards study abroad. We will help you find a program within your budget!

 INDIANA UNIVERSITY

Overseas Study

Franklin Hall 303
Bloomington IN 47405
812.855.9304

home | site map | contact

Basics
Programs
Applications
Other forms
Policies
News & Events
Contacts

Search

Welcome

For decades, the Office of Overseas Study has helped students earn IU credit by exploring educational opportunities throughout the world.

The Office of Overseas Study

- Facilitates the IU study abroad experiences of over 1,800 students on all eight Indiana University campuses,

- Offers a variety of exceptional programs chosen or developed to maintain IU's high academic standards,

- Fosters opportunities for international and cross-cultural experience,

- Gives more than $75,000 in need and merit-based scholarships annually and works to ensure programs remain affordable, and

- Provides guidance to help students integrate study abroad into their academic plans and graduate on time.

Mission Statement

The mission of the Office of Overseas Study is to promote study abroad by Indiana University students through participation in quality programs in a wide range of disciplines. The purpose is to enhance international awareness and understanding and enrich curricula on every campus of the university, as well as to expand educational opportunities abroad for students from diverse backgrounds.

As the most effective and dramatic experience by which

Announcement
Kenya Situation

IU Students Awarded
Gilman Scholarships

For Parents
Play an active role in the study abroad experience.

For Faculty & Staff
Find the information you need to work with Overseas Study.

Returning Students
Make a fresh start at IU and build on your experience abroad.

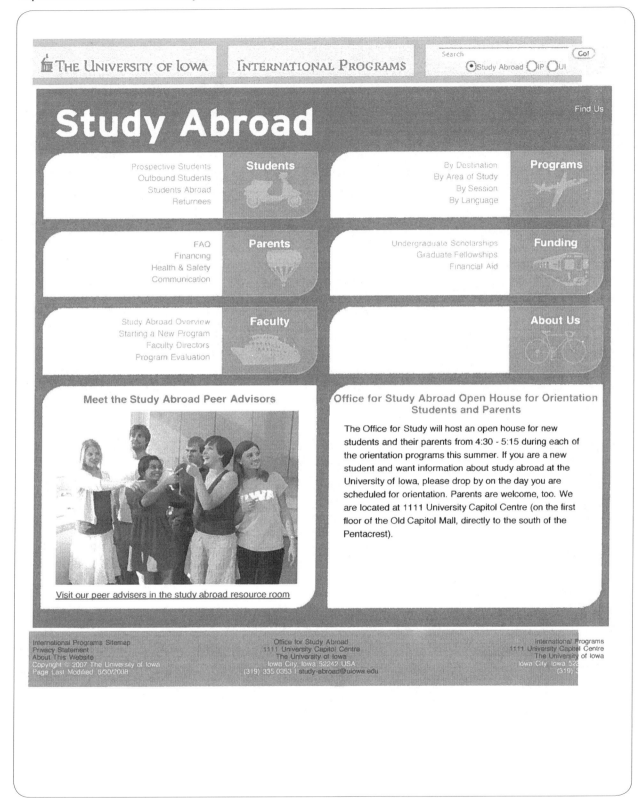

Study Abroad

Students
Prospective Students
Outbound Students
Students Abroad
Returnees

Programs
By Destination
By Area of Study
By Session
By Language

Parents
FAQ
Financing
Health & Safety
Communication

Funding
Undergraduate Scholarships
Graduate Fellowships
Financial Aid

Faculty
Study Abroad Overview
Starting a New Program
Faculty Directors
Program Evaluation

About Us

Meet the Study Abroad Peer Advisors

Visit our peer advisers in the study abroad resource room

Office for Study Abroad Open House for Orientation Students and Parents

The Office for Study will host an open house for new students and their parents from 4:30 - 5:15 during each of the orientation programs this summer. If you are a new student and want information about study abroad at the University of Iowa, please drop by on the day you are scheduled for orientation. Parents are welcome, too. We are located at 1111 University Capitol Centre (on the first floor of the Old Capitol Mall, directly to the south of the Pentacrest).

International Programs Sitemap
Privacy Statement
About This Website
Copyright © 2007 The University of Iowa
Page Last Modified 5/30/2008

Office for Study Abroad
1111 University Capitol Centre
The University of Iowa
Iowa City, Iowa 52242 USA
(319) 335 0353 | study-abroad@uiowa.edu

International Programs
1111 University Capitol Centre
The University of Iowa
Iowa City, Iowa 522
(319)

IOWA STATE UNIVERSITY: College of Design. Rome Program

http://www.design.iastate.edu/ROME/

College of Design

News | Calendar | Directory | Index   Search ___ (Go)

> About the Program
> Current News
> Fall Program
> Spring Program
> Summer program
> Campus & Facilities
> FAQ

The College of Design Rome Program offers an optional course of study for qualified students in various disciplines within the college.

The college's flagship international program has given more than 1000 students the opportunity to study in Rome since its inception in 1991. It is the only fully licensed study-abroad program in the Iowa Regents' system.

Full-semester study options are available for art and design (fall) and architecture (spring) students. In the summer an interdisciplinary program brings students together from all departments in the college. Qualified students from other institutions are also welcome to enroll in the summer session. Iowa State University faculty members and European lecturers teach students in English.

Students attend classes at our studio facilities in the historic center of Rome. In January 2005, the program moved to its new home at Palazzo Cenci-Bolognetti, a sixteenth-century edifice located in the Piazza delle Cinque Scole near the Tiber River. In addition to developing first-hand knowledge of numerous contemporary and historic sites, buildings and works of art, students gain a familiarity with the contemporary design culture of Europe through guided field trips and complete major studio projects in their design area.

Current news ɔɔ
. Grant to help LA dept., Ames address College Cre...
. Solar Decathlon team shares Interlock House conc...
. 'Decathletes' look to sun for power (ISU Solar D...
. Whiteford to lead search for College of Design d...
. Three design faculty earn promotion, tenure

Upcoming events ɔɔ
. Michael Stanley MFA Exhibition Reception
. Welcome Reception / Christian Petersen Design Aw...
. Public Forum: Dean Search
. Foreign Travel Grants Due
. College Visit w/ President and Provost

UNIVERSITY OF KENTUCKY: Office of International Affairs

http://www.uky.edu/IntlAffairs/index.htm

UK | UNIVERSITY OF KENTUCKY | ACADEMIC PROGRAMS | ATHLETICS | UK HEALTHCARE | RESEARCH | SITE INDEX | Search UK

UNIVERSITY OF KENTUCKY
Office of International Affairs

- Home
- About Us
- Forms
- Resources
- Photo Gallery
- Calendar
- Join OIA Listserv
- Give to OIA

[ ] (Search)

- Prospective/New Students
- Current Students
- J-1 Scholars
- Hiring International Faculty & Staff
- Education Abroad
- Community Programs
- UK International Links

News & Events

Information for New International Students

Optional Practical Training(OPT) 12-Month Update and 17-Month Application (6/11/08)

EA Ambassador/Assistant Applications Available

International Student Council Nomination Form

UK-Sponsored Education Abroad **Programs still taking applications:**
--Winter Caribbean Cruise Program

Health Insurance Waiver Procedure

Last Updated: June 25, 2008
Questions? Comments?
Contact: Webmaster
The University of Kentucky is an equal opportunity university.

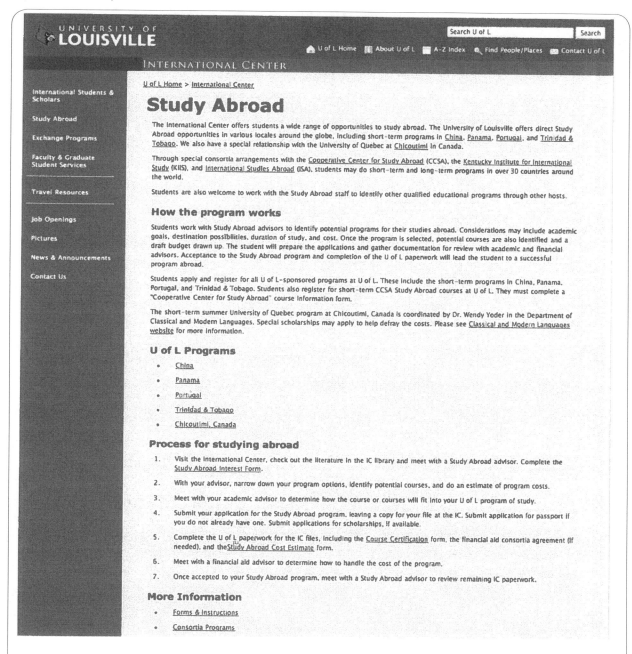

http://studyabroad.unc.edu/studyabroad.cfm

Getting Started
Find a Program
Meet the Advisors
How to Find Us
Study Abroad Guide
Quick Apply
For Parents
Scholarships/Financial Aid
Health & Safety
Minority Students (ICAMS)
Int'l Students
Mission Statement
Links
Transcript Request
Document Center
Returning Students
Report Web Errors

In the news

- ISV, AUP, Cultural Embrace Programs Not Approved for Credit
- No Delays in Issuing This Passport: Going Green Abroad
- Urgent Update on Passport Delays
- New Visa Requirements for United Kingdom

[more]

There's a whole world out there!
What are you waiting for?

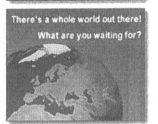

SEVILLA   PHILLIPS AMBASSADORS   SINGAPORE JOINT DEGREE PROGRAM

KING'S COLLEGE ALLIANCE   CAROLINA SOUTHEAST ASIA SUMMER PROGRAM   LORENZO DE'MEDICI

College of Arts and Sciences   Copyright 2008 UNC Study Abroad   Report problems to the webmaster

NORTH CAROLINA STATE UNIVERSITY: Design Home. Programs and Courses. Study Abroad. Prague

http://ncsudesign.org/content/index.cfm/mode/1/fuseaction/page/filename/prague.html

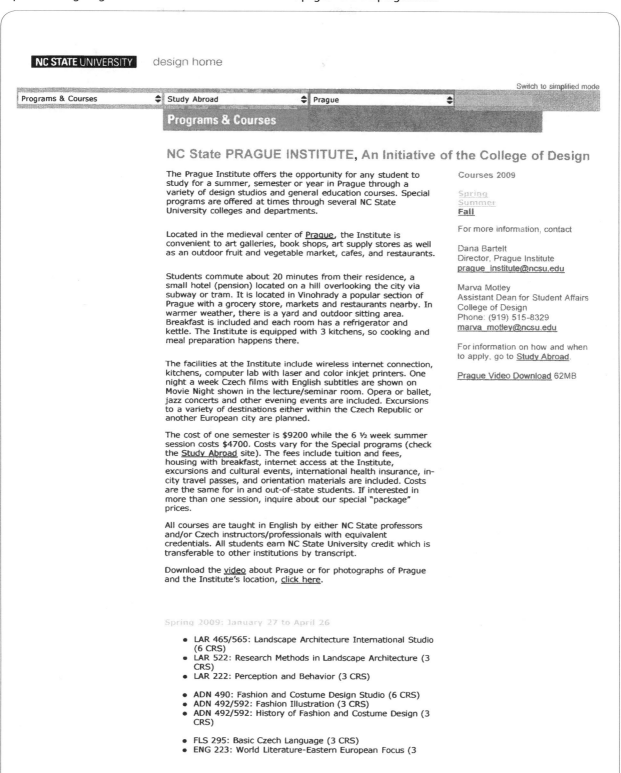

NC STATE UNIVERSITY   design home

Switch to simplified mode

Programs & Courses   Study Abroad   Prague

Programs & Courses

NC State PRAGUE INSTITUTE, An Initiative of the College of Design

The Prague Institute offers the opportunity for any student to study for a summer, semester or year in Prague through a variety of design studios and general education courses. Special programs are offered at times through several NC State University colleges and departments.

Located in the medieval center of Prague, the Institute is convenient to art galleries, book shops, art supply stores as well as an outdoor fruit and vegetable market, cafes, and restaurants.

Students commute about 20 minutes from their residence, a small hotel (pension) located on a hill overlooking the city via subway or tram. It is located in Vinohrady a popular section of Prague with a grocery store, markets and restaurants nearby. In warmer weather, there is a yard and outdoor sitting area. Breakfast is included and each room has a refrigerator and kettle. The Institute is equipped with 3 kitchens, so cooking and meal preparation happens there.

The facilities at the Institute include wireless internet connection, kitchens, computer lab with laser and color inkjet printers. One night a week Czech films with English subtitles are shown on Movie Night shown in the lecture/seminar room. Opera or ballet, jazz concerts and other evening events are included. Excursions to a variety of destinations either within the Czech Republic or another European city are planned.

The cost of one semester is $9200 while the 6 ½ week summer session costs $4700. Costs vary for the Special programs (check the Study Abroad site). The fees include tuition and fees, housing with breakfast, internet access at the Institute, excursions and cultural events, international health insurance, in-city travel passes, and orientation materials are included. Costs are the same for in and out-of-state students. If interested in more than one session, inquire about our special "package" prices.

All courses are taught in English by either NC State professors and/or Czech instructors/professionals with equivalent credentials. All students earn NC State University credit which is transferable to other institutions by transcript.

Download the video about Prague or for photographs of Prague and the Institute's location, click here.

Courses 2009

Spring
Summer
Fall

For more information, contact

Dana Bartelt
Director, Prague Institute
prague_institute@ncsu.edu

Marva Motley
Assistant Dean for Student Affairs
College of Design
Phone: (919) 515-8329
marva_motley@ncsu.edu

For information on how and when to apply, go to Study Abroad.

Prague Video Download 62MB

Spring 2009: January 27 to April 26

- LAR 465/565: Landscape Architecture International Studio (6 CRS)
- LAR 522: Research Methods in Landscape Architecture (3 CRS)
- LAR 222: Perception and Behavior (3 CRS)

- ADN 490: Fashion and Costume Design Studio (6 CRS)
- ADN 492/592: Fashion Illustration (3 CRS)
- ADN 492/592: History of Fashion and Costume Design (3 CRS)

- FLS 295: Basic Czech Language (3 CRS)
- ENG 223: World Literature-Eastern European Focus (3

NORTHWESTERN UNIVERSITY: Study Abroad

http://www.northwestern.edu/studyabroad/index.html

STUDENTS | PARENTS | ADVISERS | PROGRAMS | CALENDAR | RESEARCH | SUMMER STUDY ABROAD | FORMS | CONTACT US

" Studying abroad has opened my mind to the idea that we live in a world. Before I considered all issues from the viewpoint of the US. Studying abroad has shown me the faults that the US has, and gave me the opportunity to change the way I live back home. I have taken a greater interest in learning Spanish. I am strongly considering going back to Europe for work in the future... "

-Justin Brown
IES-Salamanca, Spain

Shadow of the Eiffel Tower
Paris, France
Taken by Katy Hitchins

Step 1: Take the mandatory Study Abroad 101 Quiz on Blackboard.

- To register for the quiz, email studyabroad@northwestern.edu with "Study Abroad 101" in the subject line. Include your name and NetID in the email.
- Be patient! Registration takes places once a week, and you will receive a confirmation email with instructions at that time. You can take the quiz as many times as needed to score a 90% or above.
- NOTE: *Students planning on applying to a Northwestern-run summer program only do NOT need to complete the Quiz and should instead consult the individual summer program pages for application instructions.*

Step 2: After successfully earning a 90% or above on the quiz, stop by the Study Abroad Office (630 Dartmouth Place) to pick up the NU Application for Permission to Study Abroad. This application is not available online and must be picked up in person. Applications for Summer 2009 and the 2009-2010 academic year will be available in early Fall 2008.

Step 3: (Strongly recommended) Schedule an appointment with a Study Abroad Adviser to discuss program options and specific concerns. For students interested in studying abroad on a Non-Northwestern summer program, this step IS required and students should plan on meeting with a study abroad advisor well in advance of the March 5 summer deadline.

Step 4: Apply to study abroad.

- June 2: Winter/Spring 2009 application deadline
- Deadlines for 2009-10 will be posted in Fall 2008.

OHIO UNIVERSITY: Education Abroad. Welcome from the Director

http://www.ohio.edu/educationabroad/info/welcomeletter.cfm

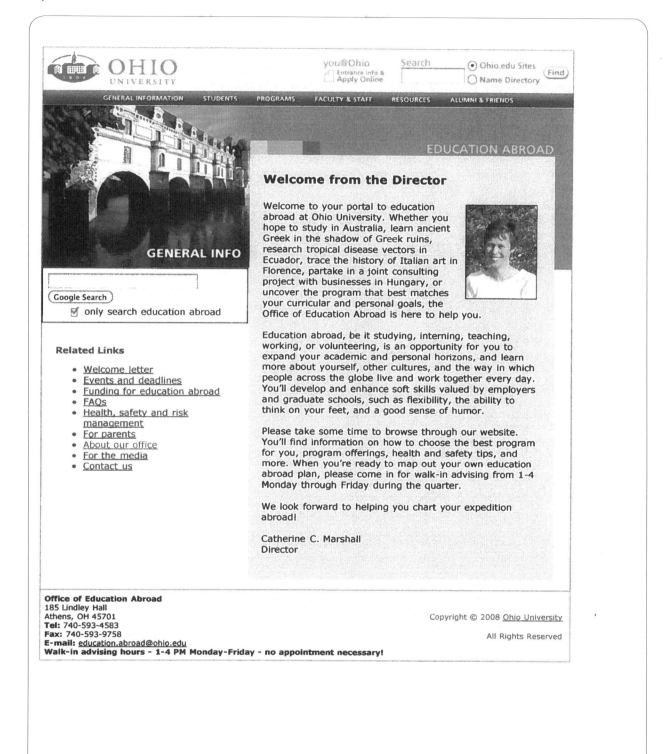

UNIVERSITY OF OKLAHOMA: Education Abroad

http://www.ou.edu/ea/home.html

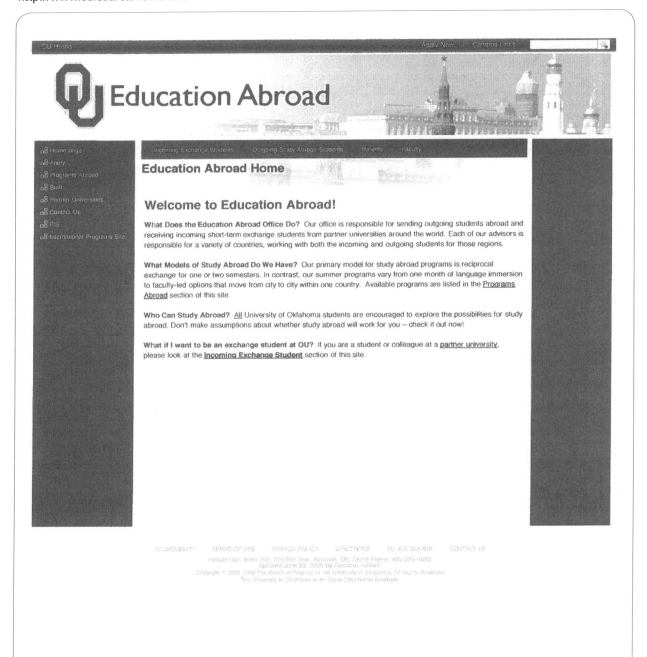

OKLAHOMA STATE UNIVERSITY: School of International Studies. Study Abroad/NSE

http://sois.okstate.edu/ieo.aspx?page=16

PURDUE UNIVERSITY: Study Abroad

http://www.studyabroad.purdue.edu

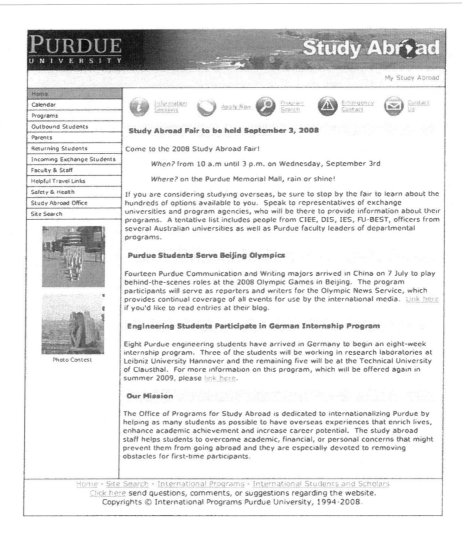

RICE UNIVERSITY: International Programs. Rice Abroad

http://abroad.rice.edu/index.cfm?fuseaction=home.main

SUABROAD
Syracuse University

LOGIN: PASSWORD: Login

INTERESTED STUDENTS :: ACCEPTED STUDENTS :: PARENTS :: FACULTY :: STUDY ABROAD ADVISORS :: ALUMNI

- University Scholars and SU Abroad
- SU Florence announces finalists in the Academic Excellence Award
- Creativity Takes Flight: Student Finds Inspiration in Study Abroad Experience
- SU Abroad students in Beijing join mock UN debate
- Photographer to address ethics, social responsibility in art at SU Florence

NEWS & INFO

WELCOME TO SU ABROAD
YOUR PLACE IN THE WORLD

- About Us
- Programs By Location
- Programs By Subject
- Summer Programs
- Short-Term Programs
- To Apply
- News & Info

[SEARCH]

SEARCH BY LOCATION

NEW: MUSLIM CULTURES

NEW CENTER: SANTIAGO, CHILE

GRADUATE PROGRAMS

Every year, students from universities across the U.S. entrust their international education to SU Abroad.

Our programs allow you to customize an international experience that meets your linguistic needs—and your professional and personal goals. Choose from exciting and challenging locations across the globe. Browse our extensive courses and programs of study that allow you to combine liberal arts and professional degree courses. Select a length of stay that works for you. You'll discover yourself as you engage with your host city through artistic collaborations and community projects, field study, internships and service learning.

You can start your explorations right here. For nearly 50 years, we have helped students from every major find their place in the world. We're ready for you.

DISCOVERY FLORENCE
FIRST-SEMESTER LIBERAL ARTS PROGRAM

SAFETY OK
SAFETY INFORMATION FOR STUDENTS AND PARENTS

Fall 2008 App Deadlines:

Applications still being accepted on a space-available basis. (Note: Some World Partner programs still available)

◎ Search Programs and Courses

◎ Request More Information

◎ Attend an Information Session

◎ Apply Online

TEXAS TECH UNIVERSITY: Study Abroad

http://www.studyabroad.ttu.edu/

UNIVERSITY OF VIRGINIA: International Studies Office. Study Abroad

http://www.studyabroad.virginia.edu/

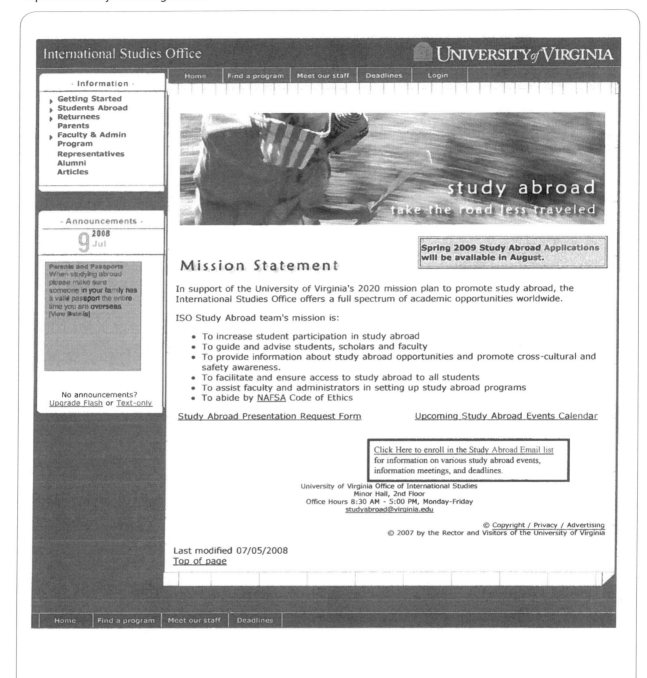

UNIVERSITY OF VIRGINIA: Semester at Sea. Academic Community

http://www.semesteratsea.org/academic-life/overview/academic-community.php

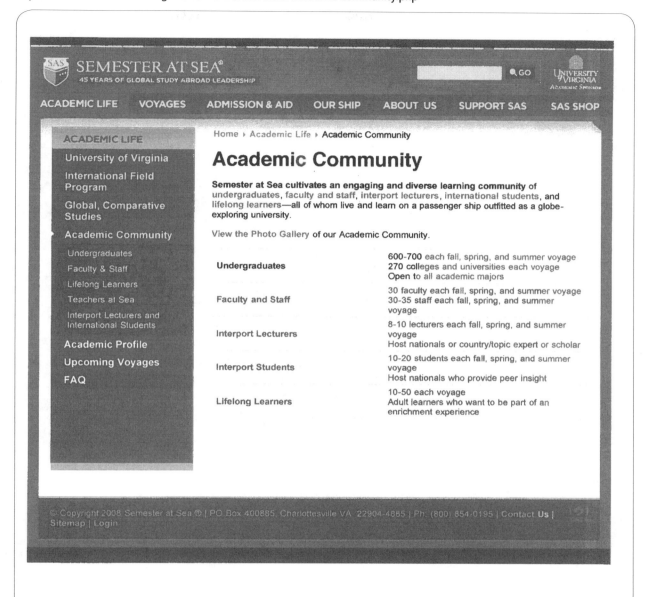

http://www.ip.wsu.edu/education_abroad/

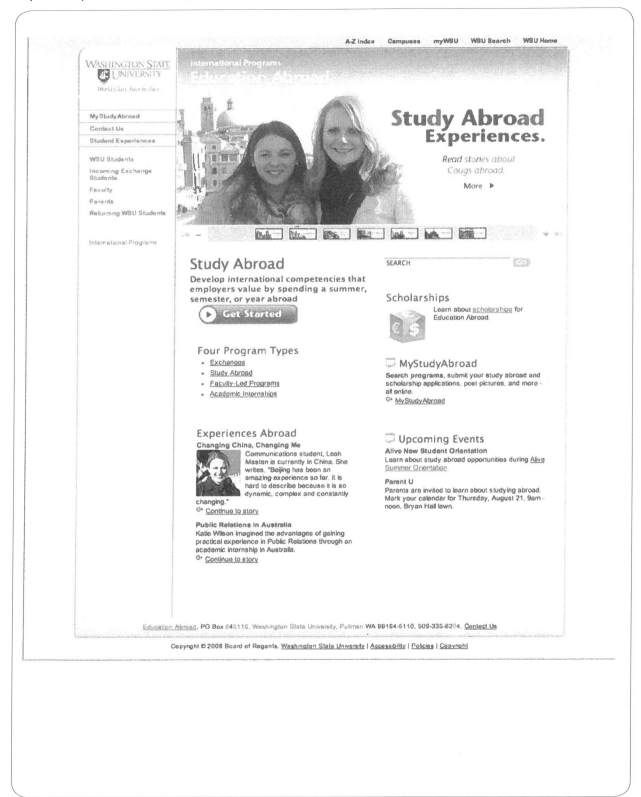

UNIVERSITY OF WESTERN ONTARIO: Student Development Services. Exchange Programs: Leaving Western

http://www.sdc.uwo.ca/int/exchange/index.html?outgoing

Text-only View

Contact Us | About SDS | Search

The University of
Western Ontario
Student Development Services

Exchange Programs: Leaving Western

- Welcome
- News and Updates
- Why Study on Exchange?
- Benefits
- Eligibility
- Exchange vs. Studying Abroad
- Information Sessions & Office hours
- Exchange Destinations
- Application Process
- Criteria for Selection & Special Considerations
- Pre-Departure Orientation
- Passports & Visas
- Health & Safety
- Scholarships & Other Funding
- Travel & Tourism Information
- International Opportunities Fair
- Contact Us

Learn more about the International Exchange Program by speaking with students who have studied on exchange, as well as students who are here at Western on exchange.

APPLY NOW!

Welcome to Western's International Exchange Program. Our exchange agreements with partner institutions across the globe provide Western students with the opportunity to study at more than 50 universities around the world. Western students can study in one of the following countries:

- Australia
- Denmark
- Finland
- France
- Germany
- Hong Kong
- Japan
- Mexico
- The Netherlands
- Singapore
- Sweden
- United Kingdom
- United States

News and Updates

The Honourable Company of Freeman of the City of London, England Scholarship
Awarded to a graduate or undergraduate student in any program of any year who has been accepted to pursue course work or significant scholarly activity for a minimum of three months at a university or college in Greater London Authority or the City of London, England. Preference will be given to graduate students whose scholarly pursuits would benefit from the opportunity to travel and live in London, England. However, undergraduate students applying for an approved exchange program, study abroad or other international experience to take place at a university or college in London, England also may apply. The Honourable Company will endeavour to introduce the student to a Guild event in the City of London, England.

Yale University

Yale Summer Session
Same Veritas. More Lux.

Summer Session Home

Study Abroad

Basic Information

Global Summer Program

Programs ▸

How to Apply ▸

Study Abroad Handbook

ISA Information

Academic and Financial Information ▸

Student Life ▸

University Resources ▸

Information for Faculty

Contact YSS Study Abroad

Study Abroad

Yale Summer Session Study Abroad offers students the intellectual challenge they expect from Yale in classrooms that spill out onto the streets of the world. First-hand experience of foreign cultures is a basic component of a Yale education: it not only complements the student's academic study of international topics, but is also fundamental to the student's own personal development as a global citizen. We hope that studying abroad with Yale Summer Session will mark the beginning of a lifetime of encounters with members of the new global community.

Check out our photo contest winners from YSS 2007!

Library Services for Study Abroad Programs

http://www.gwu.edu/gelman/service/offcampus/

Library Services > Off-Campus

Library Services for Off-Campus/Online Programs

You are an off-campus or online student if . . . you are enrolled in online programs or programs at locations other than Foggy Bottom, Mt. Vernon, and Virginia Campus. See GW Off-Campus Programs, GW College of Professional Studies, GW Summer Online, Study Abroad GW Students for more information.

Start Your Research: Choose Your Task

Got an article citation? E-Journals finds it online — Look for a specific article or journal title online. If it isn't available, search for the journal title in the ALADIN Catalog so that you can request it. Help!

Find books & journals: ALADIN Catalog — Search the catalog for journal or book titles. You **won't** find individual articles in the catalog. Click on **Advanced Search** to search for a topic.

Request books & articles — Request books or articles that aren't available online. **Click the red button for instructions.** Where do I send my books back?

Find articles: ALADIN Research Portal — Search for articles for your topic through all Gelman's databases Gelman subscribes to. Help!

Check your library account: MyALADIN — Renew your books online, download articles you requested, check the status of your requests. Help!

Easy bibliographies: RefWorks — Keep track of your sources and in-text citations. RefWorks makes it easier to create bibliographies & footnotes. Help!

How to use the library: DoItYourself@Gelman — Learn how to use the library without having to ask.

Choose Your Program

Business Administration & Tourism Administration

Educational Leadership & Admin., Educational Admin. & Policy Studies

Engineering Management & Mgmt. Information Systems

Education & Counseling

Electrical & Systems Engineering

Human Resources

Paola Ceccarini
Distance Education Librarian
202-994-1342
AIM: caloap

off-campus access | faculty | visiting gelman | prepare your thesis/dissertation | dissertation express

THE GEORGE WASHINGTON UNIVERSITY
WASHINGTON DC

Last modified: Thursday, 19-Jun-2008 11:44:23 EDT

GEORGE WASHINGTON UNIVERSITY: Do It Yourself@Gelman. Request Items

http://www.gwu.edu/gelman/service/offcampus/diy/ocpcls.html

Library Services > Off-Campus > DIY home

Do It Yourself@Gelman
Request Items (Off-campus/online Programs)

Use it for: Requesting books and articles, not available electronically, from Gelman, Consortium Libraries, or any other libraries.

 Watch It!   Print It!

Why use it? Because you can get books and articles at your doorstep or to your desktop for free!

Items IN the ALADIN Catalog
Step 1

In the ALADIN Catalog, click on the title of the book/journal you need for one of the libraries that has it. The catalog record screen appears. I need help understanding this record.

Step 2

- For a book, look at "Status" under "Availability" to make sure that it's not checked out.
- For a journal, look under "Library has" to make sure the year you need is available.

Step 3

Click on the link "Request through Consortium Loan Services (CLS)". In the new window log into ALADIN. First-time user?

Step 4

- On the request form, under **"Library for Pickup"** select **"GW Off-campus Programs."**
- Under "University ID" type your GWid# or GWorld card barcode.
- For a **journal article**, fill in the boxes with all the requested data from the article.
- **Type your delivery address** in the "Comment" box. Click "Submit Request."

Step 5

- A confirmation message appears. Disregard any message you receive that says "the book is available for pick up at "GW Off-Campus Programs."
- **Books** will be shipped to your home address, and you'll need to ship them back to Gelman.
- You'll receive **articles** electronically via email.

GEORGE WASHINGTON UNIVERSITY: Do It Yourself@Gelman. Request Items

http://www.gwu.edu/gelman/service/offcampus/diy/ocpcls.html

Items NOT in the ALADIN Catalog
Step 1

If you can't find your title in the ALADIN Catalog, request it through Interlibrary Loan. I need help placing an ILL request.

Need Help?

Did You Know?

- Gelman Library CLS
  Tel.: 202-994-1306
  E-mail: libcls@gwu.edu

- Gelman Library Reference Desk
  Tel.: 202-994-6048
  E-mail: refdesk@gwu.edu

Was This Helpful?

#&*%!

Can't tell if the book is available?

Before you request a book from GM or GT make sure it's available. In the GM or GT catalog record click on the URL link (George Mason or Georgetown Holdings). If the book is not checked out, click the back arrow and make the request, Step 3.

THE GEORGE
WASHINGTON
UNIVERSITY
WASHINGTON DC

Last modified: Thursday, June 19, 2008 15:31:41 PM

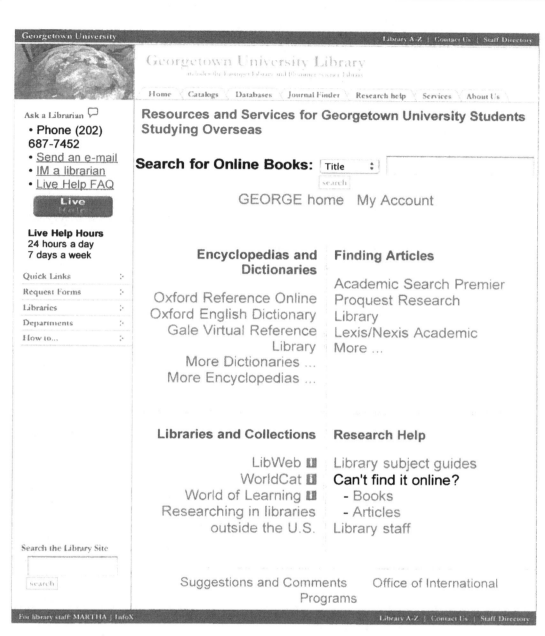

37th and N Streets, N.W., Washington, D.C., 20057 | (202) 687-7452

Copyright 2003 Georgetown University Libraries

Georgetown University   Library A-Z | Contact Us | Staff Directory

Georgetown University Library
includes the Lauinger Library and Bioscience Science Library

Home   Catalogs   Databases   Journal Finder   Research help   Services   About Us

Ask a Librarian 💬
• Phone (202) 687-7452
• Send an e-mail
• IM a librarian
• Live Help FAQ

Live
Help

Live Help Hours
24 hours a day
7 days a week

Quick Links   :·
Request Forms   :·
Libraries   :·
Departments   :·
How to...   :·

Search the Library Site

[search]

Resources and Services for Georgetown University Students Studying Overseas

Search for Online Books: [Title ▼] [_____] [search]
GEORGE home   My Account

Back to Overseas Main Page

Obtaining Books from Georgetown

We are unable to lend print copies of books from the Library's collections. However, we may be able to make copies of selected pages or of a chapter.

To request pages to be copied, please fill out an interlibrary loan (ILL) form for a book and note:

1. Chapter or pages to be copied.
2. You are an overseas student

Questions? Email the interlibrary loan department.
Looking for articles?

Suggestions and Comments   Office of International Programs

For library staff: MARTHA | InfoX   Library A-Z | Contact Us | Staff Directory

37th and N Streets, N.W., Washington, D.C., 20057 | (202) 687-7452
Copyright 2003 Georgetown University Libraries

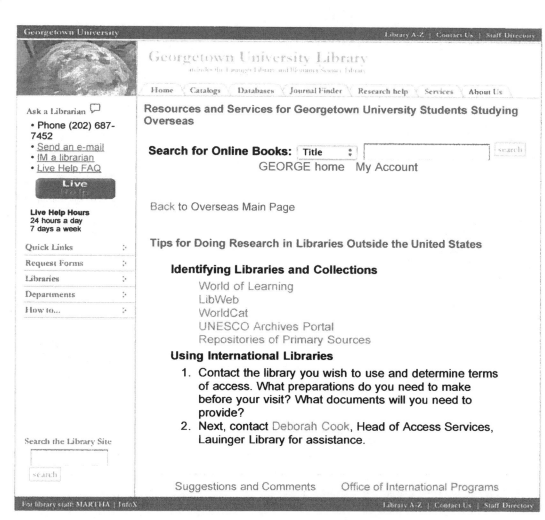

UNIVERSITY OF HAWAI'I AT MANOA: Study Abroad Center. Resources

http://www.studyabroad.org/resources.htm

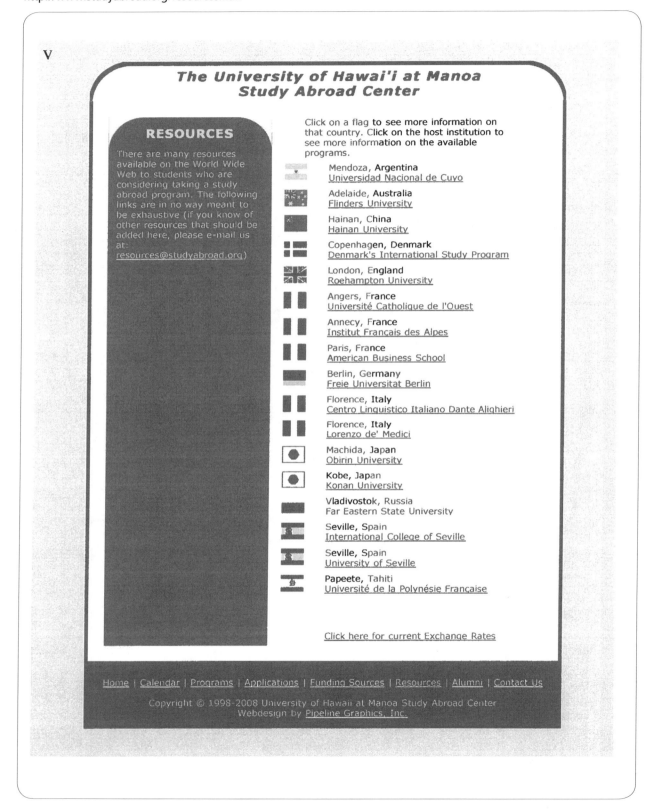

V

The University of Hawai'i at Manoa Study Abroad Center

RESOURCES

There are many resources available on the World Wide Web to students who are considering taking a study abroad program. The following links are in no way meant to be exhaustive (if you know of other resources that should be added here, please e-mail us at: resources@studyabroad.org)

Click on a flag to see more information on that country. Click on the host institution to see more information on the available programs.

Mendoza, **Argentina**
Universidad Nacional de Cuyo

Adelaide, **Australia**
Flinders University

Hainan, China
Hainan University

Copenhagen, **Denmark**
Denmark's International Study Program

London, **England**
Roehampton University

Angers, France
Université Catholique de l'Ouest

Annecy, France
Institut Français des Alpes

Paris, France
American Business School

Berlin, Germany
Freie Universitat Berlin

Florence, **Italy**
Centro Linguistico Italiano Dante Alighieri

Florence, **Italy**
Lorenzo de' Medici

Machida, **Japan**
Obirin University

Kobe, Japan
Konan University

Vladivostok, Russia
Far Eastern State University

Seville, Spain
International College of Seville

Seville, Spain
University of Seville

Papeete, Tahiti
Université de la Polynésie Française

Click here for current Exchange Rates

Home | Calendar | Programs | Applications | Funding Sources | Resources | Alumni | Contact Us

Copyright © 1998-2008 University of Hawaii at Manoa Study Abroad Center
Webdesign by Pipeline Graphics, Inc.

UNIVERSITY OF ILLINOIS AT URBANA-CHAMPAIGN: Diversity & Multicultural Information. Library Resources

http://www.library.uiuc.edu/ugl/diversity/

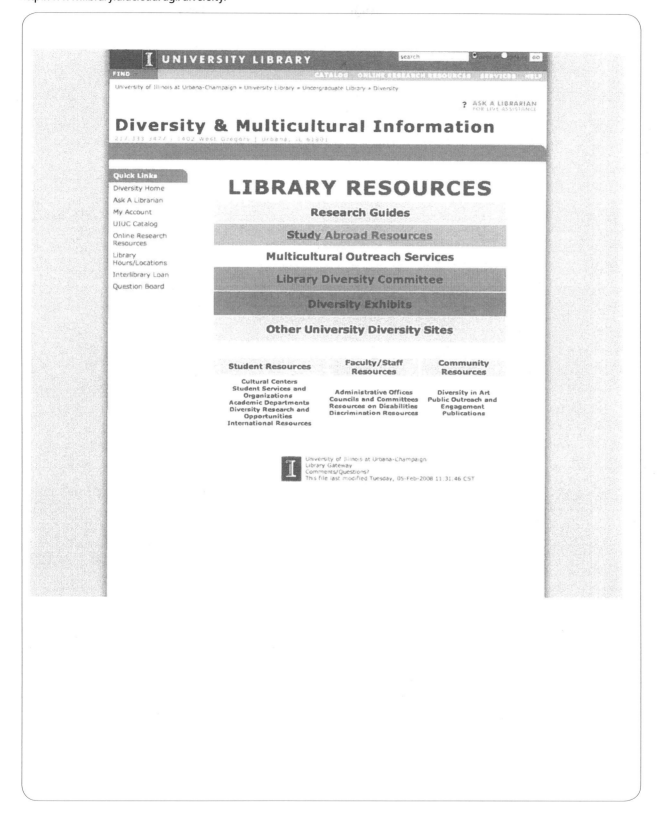

Study Abroad Resources

The University of Illinois has a large student population who study abroad during their university years. Researching and learning about the country or area before studying abroad is an important preparation step. The Undergraduate Library has a wide range of books, DVD's, videos, and other resources for students who will study abroad. More resources can also be found at the **Study Abroad Office**.

- **Africa**
- **Asia**
- **Australia**
- **Austria**
- **Brazil**
- **Canada**
- **Central America, Mexico, and the Caribbean**
- **China**
- **Europe**
- **France**
- **Germany**
- **Illinois**
- **Ireland**
- **Italy**
- **New Zealand**
- **Russia and Eastern Europe**
- **Southwest Asia** (including the Middle East)
- **South America**
- **Spain**
- **United Kingdom**
- **United States of America**

Return to Top

 **INDIANA UNIVERSITY**
BLOOMINGTON

LIBRARIES > Reference

| Faculty | Graduate Students | Undergraduates | Visitors |

Resource ▸ | Services ▸ | Subjects ▸ | Search | Go

IUCAT | Libraries & Hours | Ask a Librarian

Research Seminars
Internet Quick Reference
Research Guides
Distance Education
» Libraries in Indiana
» DE class pages
EndNote
Have You Been Cited?
How to Cite
Copyright and Fair Use
More about the department

Contact Information ▼

Department Head: Mary Strow

Location: Wells Library E159
1320 East Tenth Street
Bloomington, Indiana 47405
Phone: (812) 855-8028
E-mail: libref
Staff: View Staff

» View Map of IUB Libraries
» Building Access

Distance Education Home

 Short video about Distance Education services at the IU Libraries
This file requires the plug-in: Quicktime. If you need to download a free copy of Quicktime, click here.

Distributed (Distance) Education Library Services are for you if you:

- are enrolled in IU Bloomington courses but not currently residing in the Bloomington area.
- are taking IU Bloomington courses abroad
- are PhD candidates enrolled for dissertation credit
- are an IUB faculty member not currently in the Bloomington area.

If you are an IU student from another campus, please contact the library at your home campus for assistance.

Need research assistance? **Ask a Librarian:**

- by e-mail (libdist@indiana.edu)
  by live chat or instant messaging (IM) with a librarian
- on our toll-free phone number: (888) 258-6977 from the U.S., Canada, and the Caribbean
- or come to the Wells Library Reference Department if you happen to be in Bloomington.

Getting Started with your research: Here's all you need to use our library resources and services:

- You must have an IUB *Network ID/Password* to access our library resources.
- Request a *Library Barcode*

Forms and Policies for getting IUB Libraries books and articles delivered to your home or computer

Finding Information: Databases, IUCAT, and other information sources available through IUB

Interactive Tutorials for Library Research (online tutorials)

Tutorial for finding a book in IUCAT

How to Cite Print and Electronic Sources in APA and MLA styles

Writing Help (Writing Tutorial Services): includes How to Write a Thesis Statement, How to Avoid Plagiarism, How to Evaluate Information, and more ...

Having trouble connecting to our resources? Here's our getting connected page.

Instructors: Please contact librsvp@indiana.edu for placing materials on electronic reserves (E-reserve)

Related Links

Libraries Around the State: You may have a need to use libraries closer to you. Check here for libraries in Indiana near you. Sites include searchable online catalogs.

Walden University students: see **Library Services for Walden University**

Mission Statement:

The Indiana University Bloomington Libraries have a responsibility to provide library services to our distance learners. It is the Libraries' mission to provide access to as many resources as possible to support curriculum-related teaching, research, and scholarly communication to our off-campus students.

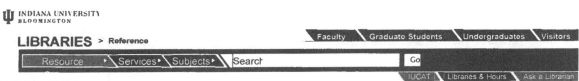

Research Seminars
Internet Quick Reference
Research Guides
Distance Education
EndNote
Have You Been Cited?
How to Cite
Copyright and Fair Use
More about the department

Contact Information ▼

Department Head: Mary
Strow

Location: Wells Library
E159
1320 East Tenth Street
Bloomington, Indiana
47405
Phone: (812) 855-8028
E-mail: libref
Staff: View Staff

» View Map of IUB
Libraries
» Building Access

**Recommended
Resources** ►

Useful Links ►

Distance Education Document and Book Delivery

Requesting Books and Articles
Only books owned by the IU-Bloomington libraries will be sent. Check IUCAT to determine if one of the IU-Bloomington libraries owns the book. To request books and articles, go to https://www.dds.iub.edu/logon.html. Log on with your network ID and password. Scroll down to "Distance Education Service Requests."

Loan Periods
Graduate students may borrow circulating materials for 120 days. Undergraduate students may borrow circulating materials for 45 days. There are exceptions (e.g., books from the Undergraduate Library circulate for 14 days to all categories of borrowers.)

Recalls
Books are subject to be recalled (returned to the library earlier than the due date) if requested by another person. In this case, the book MUST BE RETURNED (or postmarked) BY THE RECALL DUE DATE, or a fine of $25 will be assessed.

Renewals
A book may be renewed if another person has not requested it. Renewals may be made by phone (812) 855-4673, electronically, or in person. Renewals will NOT be accepted by fax.

Delivery
All loaned materials will be delivered to your home address, your post office box, or the address on your request form via US Media Rate. Photocopied material can be retrieved below the location where you entered your requests, by clicking on "View/Download Electronically Delivered Requests." Delivery of Bloomington-owned materials usually takes one to two weeks, so plan accordingly. Articles that have to be obtained from another library or that must be delivered outside the U.S. will take longer. *(We do not borrow books from other libraries.)*

Returning Materials
Materials may be returned in person, by U.S. mail or Courier. *The borrower is responsible for the safe return of materials to the library. The borrower will be charged for any fines related to materials that are lost in the mail. It is strongly suggested that you insure any materials you return for at least $100.* The postmark is considered the return date. Please mail to: Customer and Access Services Dept., Main Library, E164, Indiana University, Bloomington, IN 47405.

Charges
There are no charges for borrowing books or receiving articles at this time. However, the borrower is responsible for the cost of return.

Fines and Fees
Overdue fines are $.25 per day per book. There is a $25 fine for recalled books that are received or postmarked after the recall due date. Documents/articles are $5 each if fax service is requested. Fees will be assessed for lost or damaged materials. All fines and fees will be billed through the IU Bursar's Office.

IUB Home | Libraries Privacy Policy | Sitemap | News & Events | About IUB Libraries | Outages and Downtime | Comments to libref@indiana.edu | Print

 INDIANA UNIVERSITY
BLOOMINGTON

LIBRARIES > Document Delivery Services

| Resource ▸ | Service ▸ | Subject ▸ | Searc | | Go | ate | Undergraduate | Visitors |

IUCAT | Libraries & Hours | Ask a Librarian

Contact Information ▼

**Department
Head:** Rita Rogers

Location: Indiana
University Libraries
1320 E. 10th Street
Bloomington, Indiana
47405
Phone: (812) 855-
4397
Fax: (812) 855-8229
E-mail: Borrowing: libill
Staff: View Staff

Department: Customer
and Access Services

» View Map of IUB
Libraries

**Recommended
Resources** ▸

Useful Links ▸

Document Delivery Services-- FAQ

Table of Contents:

Who May Use This Service?

Document Delivery/Interlibrary loan is a service offered
through the Herman B Wells Library Customer and Access
Services Department to Indiana University - Bloomington
faculty, students, and staff who are engaged in research.
The conditions of this service are set by the Interlibrary
Loan Code of the American Library Association and by
regulations of individual lending libraries.
Time Required

The time to receive an item varies; 70% of articles and
55% of books are received in 7 days or less. When
several libraries must be contacted before an available
copy is located, the process may take longer. Requests
that must be sent internationally usually take considerably
longer than this average.
<< top of page

Duration of Loans

The loan period for borrowed material is set by the lending
library and is indicated on a date due slip in the book. The
maximum loan period is given; please use the material
within that time period. In the interest of maintaining
good relations with lending libraries, due dates must be
honored. Returnable material will be checked out through
the Herman B Wells Library Research Collections
Circulation Counter and should be returned there.
Requestors will be billed for non-returned overdue items
and library privileges may be suspended until materials are
returned. If a borrower continually disregards due dates,
it may be necessary to refuse further service.
<< top of page

Restrictions on Use

Indiana University Libraries is bound by any restriction on use imposed by the lending library. Some libraries require that the materials they lend be used in the borrowing library only. Some do not allow photocopying. Some require the signature of readers of unpublished dissertations. The requestor should not let others use the borrowed books unless special arrangements have been made.
<< top of page

Recently Published Books

It is often difficult to borrow recently published books on interlibrary loan because they are in demand at the libraries owning them. You may wish to suggest the purchase of such materials for the IUL collections. **<< top of page**

Other Policy Information

As a general policy, we will not borrow any book available in a library on the Bloomington campus. Items which cannot be located by those libraries may be requested through Document Delivery Services.

Please submit Document Delivery requests through our web site at https://www.dds.iub.edu/illiad/logon.html. If you experience difficulties, please call (812) 855-6549 and ask for assistance.

 Photocopied material can be received via our web site. An e-mail message will be sent to the requestor with instruction as to how to retrieve the document. Loans will be delivered to Campus Mail addresses or notification for picking up an item will be sent sent to your IU e-mail address. Overdues and recalls will also be sent to your e-mail account.

Registering to use the IUB Document Delivery Services interlibrary loan requesting system:

> **Go to:**
> **http://www.dds.iub.edu/illiad/logon.html**
>   OR
> From the Libraries Home Page choose
>   Library Services
>   Borrow, Renew & Request
>   Request Materials IUB Libraries Do Not Own (ILL)
>   Submit a Request
> The Indiana University Document Delivery Services Logon Screen appears (can be Bookmarked/added to Favorites).
> First time users should enter their Network ID and Password to fill out their profile:

First name (required)
Last name (required)
Library ID Number – 14 digits (required) -- this is your library barcode number
E-Mail address: use the < >@indiana.edu email
Preferred Article Method: dropdown box has choices of Electronic Delivery or
    Mail to Address. Most will be Electronic Delivery (requestors are notified
    via email when they have an article to view and given a PIN number for access).
Preferred Loan Delivery Method: This is for items that must be returned.
Mailing Address (required)
Secondary Mailing Address (Alternate Mailing Location)
Status: (required) Options are Faculty, Graduate, Undergraduate, Staff
Department: This dropdown box contains the same departments as Worldcat's FirstSearch.

(return to top)

Logon

After the registration information is filled in, requestors will be prompted to logon with their Network ID (username)and password. This will take the requestor to the Main Menu.

(return to top)

MAIN MENU OPTIONS

 Request Article Delivery
Request a copy of an article owned only in print on the Bloomington campus, to be delivered electronically. An email notification will be sent to you when the document is available.

 InterLibrary Loan Requests
Request an article or book not owned by the IU Library system.

 **Distance Education Service Requests**
For IU Bloomington enrolled students living remotely.

Review Requests

- **view and edit your outstanding requests, including detailed request information and statuses.**
- view items that you have received for web delivery.
- view items that you have checked out along with due dates and a method to renew your loan.

- view your completed requests.
- view items that have been cancelled either by you or the InterLibrary Loan staff. You may resubmit these items with more complete and/or accurate information.

Review Personal Information
modify your personal information, including address, phone number, e-mail address and delivery preferences.

If you have questions:
    Email: libill@indiana.edu
    Phone: 855-6549
<< top of page

IUB Home | Libraries Privacy Policy | Sitemap | News & Events | About IUB Libraries | Outages and Downtime | Comments to libref@indiana.edu | Print

IU INDIANA UNIVERSITY
BLOOMINGTON

Document Delivery Services Logon Screen

Including Request Article Delivery

Status: *Enter your **Indiana University username and password** below.*
Then press the Logon *button to continue.*

First-time users will be prompted for delivery information. This information can be edited by the user.

Enter your Username:

Enter your Password:

Click Button to Logon: (Logon)

IU DDS Frequently asked questions

Indiana University Libraries Home

Request assistance/Report a problem

© 1996, 1998 *Virginia Tech Intellectual Properties, Inc.*
© 1998, 1999, 2000 *Atlas Systems, Inc.*

IOWA STATE UNIVERSITY: Distance Learning

http://www.lib.iastate.edu/class/distlearn/distlearn_main.html

IOWA STATE UNIVERSITY

▶ Text Version
▶ Help

Distance Learning

Library Catalog | Find articles | Library Information | How do I..? | Ask a Librarian

Collections | **Service Areas** | Classes & Tours | **Arts**

Circulation | Request Forms | Interlibrary Loan | Reference | Media Center | Special Collections | University Archives | Branch Facilities | Other Library Service Areas

Reserve | WebCT | CDE | Contact Us

Distance Learning

These pages are designed to help distance learning students connect to the many resources and services the Library offers. The menu below directs you to the main starting points for finding information, doing research, and getting help. Any library user who is working away from the Library can also benefit from the information here.

Get Connected

ISUCard, Library PIN, Off-campus access & more

Find Articles

Learn how to Find Articles tutorial, Indexes & Abstracts, Get what you need, & more

Find Books & More

ISU Library Catalog, Finding e-books, WorldCat, Get what you need, & more

Guides & Tutorials

Links to relevant tutorials, style guides, study support, & more

For Faculty

Reserves, Directory of subject librarians, and other ISU links

Library Information & Other Links

Visiting the ISU Library, and more

Printer-friendly version | e-Library entrance | Site Search | Site map | Top

▶ Text Version
▶ Help

Library Catalog   Find articles   Library Information   How do I..?   Ask a Librarian

Collections   Service Areas   Classes & Tours   Arts

Circulation | Request Forms | Interlibrary Loan | Reference | Media Center | Special
Collections | University Archives | Branch Facilities | Other Library Service Areas

Reserve   WebCT   CDE   Contact Us

Distance Learning

· Get connected
· **Find articles**
· Find books & more
· Guides & tutorials
· For faculty
· Library information
  & other links

Find Articles

Learn How to Find Articles -- this handy tutorial covers everything you need to know about finding full-text articles from the ISU e-Library, as well as how to get articles the ISU Library doesn't own.

Indexes & Abstracts -- these indexes will help you find articles on just about any topic. Many of the indexes include a description, letting you know the subject areas and years that are covered. Make sure to read the Find Articles tutorial if you need general help. If you're not sure which index to choose for your topic, you can always Ask a Librarian!

e-Journals list -- you can also browse the list of full-text e-journals; many of these will have their own unique search system. See the Find Articles tutorial if you need help in finding articles by browsing e-journals.

Get what you need! You'll find many of our articles full-text and online, as described above. By using Interlibrary Loan, you can also request articles that the ISU Library **doesn't** own be sent to you, for free. To use Interlibrary Loan, you'll need your ISUCard. For a fee, you can use Document Delivery, to **pay** to have copies of print articles the Library owns (but that are not full-text online) be sent to you.

Printer-friendly version | e-Library entrance | Site Search | Site map |
Top

Send questions or comments about this page
Last modified: Thursday, 17-Apr-2008 09:26:54 CDT
Copyright © 2000-2008, Iowa State University. All rights reserved.

IOWA STATE UNIVERSITY: Distance Learning. Find Books & More

http://www.lib.iastate.edu/class/distlearn/find_books.html

e-Library — IOWA STATE UNIVERSITY

▶ Text Version
▶ Help

Library Catalog   Find articles   Library Information   How do I..?   Ask a Librarian

Collections   Service Areas   Classes & Tours   Arts
Library Instruction Program I Courses A-Z I Library 160 I Instruction Commons I Reserve I
Distance Learning I Workshops & Tutorials I Library Tours

Reserve   WebCT   CDE   Contact Us

Distance Learning

* Get connected
* Find articles
* **Find books & more**
* Guides & tutorials
* For faculty
* Library information & other links

Find Books & More

ISU Library Catalog -- use the ISU Library Catalog to find books and much more in our collections. To find *only* electronic books, search the Library Catalog using a **General Keyword** search, and the terms such as:

electronic book and business	*will find e-books on business topics*
electronic books and education	*will find e-books on education topics*

Another way to find electronic books in the ISU online collections is to browse by collections. Once you have an active ISUCard and have set your Library PIN, you can also login to use the My Account feature within the ISU Library catalog. This allows you to create and save lists, see what you have checked out, and so on.

Google Book Search - allows you to search online for books in virtually any subject area. Includes excerpted reviews, occasional full-text (especially for non-copyrighted books) or limited "pre-views" of other books, and powerful full-text search ("search in this book") features. Also includes direct links for purchasing books from Amazon, Barnes & Noble, and other online vendors, as well as direct links to WorldCat (see below) for finding books in libraries nearest you.

NetLibrary is a growing collection of electronic books available via the ISU Library, with an emphasis in computer science, business, and education. Note that you do need to set up an account within NetLibrary before you can use it. If you can't come to the ISU campus to set up your account, you can email staff at the ISU Library's Circulation Desk and set up your account that way.

WorldCat -- use this free database to find books, dissertations, and more in thousands of library collections worldwide. You can find materials in

IOWA STATE UNIVERSITY: Distance Learning. Find Books & More

http://www.lib.iastate.edu/class/distlearn/find_books.html

libraries closest to you! Alternatively, you can use the ISU Library's version of WorldCat, which will allow you to use an Interlibrary Loan link to request items.

Get what you need! You'll find a number of books full-text and online, as described above. By using Interlibrary Loan, you can also request to borrow books that the ISU Library **doesn't** own be sent to you, for free. To use Interlibrary Loan, you'll need an active ISUCard. By using Document Delivery, you can **pay** to have books the Library owns but that are not full-text online be sent to you.

Printer-friendly version | e-Library entrance | Site Search | Site map | Top

Send questions or comments about this page
Last modified: Thursday, 17-Apr-2008 09:24:21 CDT
Copyright © 2000-2008, Iowa State University. All rights reserved.

UNIVERSITY OF
LOUISVILLE

UofL Home   Blackboard   GroupWise   ULink

LIBRARIES : DISTANCE LEARNING LIBRARY SERVICES

About DLLS   Databases   Subject Guides   Forms   Evaluation   Help

Greetings!

U of L distance education programs currently eligible for Distance Learning Library Services (DLLS) are listed under the tabs above.

The following library services are available for University of Louisville distance learners using their ULink username & password:

- research assistance to distance education students & faculty
- locate & retrieve items from U of L library collection or other universities
- delivery of library resources not available immediately online
- remote access to library assignments by course professors
- remote access to electronic databases of library resources for self-directed research

We look forward to serving your library research needs.

Melissa Crain, Coordinator
Office of Distance Learning Library Services
University of Louisville
dlls@louisville.edu

Distance Learning Library Services | University Libraries | University of Louisville | Louisville, KY 40292 USA
About Us | E-mail | Phone: 502-852-8745 or 1-800-334-8635 x8745 | Fax: 502-852-8743

© 2008 University of Louisville. All rights reserved.
UofL A-Z Index | People Finder | Contact UofL

Libraries & Collections | How Do I...? | Hours | Catalog | E-Research Tools | E-Journal Finder | Need Help?

DISTANCE EDUCATION LIBRARY SERVICES

Distance Students

Requesting Materials
Home and online delivery
of books and articles

E-reserves
Online class readings
(Requires Onyen and
password)

Libraries in Your Area
(Requires One Card)

Faculty & Coordinators

Requesting Materials
Home and online delivery
of books and articles

Course Support
Library services to
support instruction

Reciprocal Borrowing
Faculty library privileges
at other universities

Researchers @ a Distance

Requesting Materials
Delivery of select
materials

Using Libraries Abroad
Help with research in
specific countries

Connecting Online and In Person

Use your Onyen and password to
access library e-resources. If you are
taking self-paced classes through the
Friday Center and do not have an
Onyen, you will use your PID to get
access.

Contact Angela or Davis Circulation if
you are having difficulty getting access.

Plan a visit to the Chapel Hill campus
libraries by checking here for Hours,
Directions, Parking, and more.

Researching

Finding articles in a specific database

Finding a specific journal online

Searching for E-books

Basic article search

You may find the searching and articles
sections of the Introduction to Library
Research tutorial helpful for refining
your research.

Program-Specific Resources

Education

Information and Library Science

Journalism and Mass Communication

Social Work - General

Social Work - Research Methods

TransAtlantic Masters Program

Distance Librarian

Angela Bardeen

Phone: 919-962-1151

bardeen@email.unc.edu

AIM: angebrarian

Chat with Angela

Available

More Help

Davis Reference
919-962-1151

Davis Circulation
919-962-1053

Health Sciences Library
919-962-0800

More chat and email
options

Home | Hours | Search This Site | UNC Home

Website comments or questions: Library Web Team
Suggestions on Library Services? Give us your feedback.
URL: http://www.lib.unc.edu/de/index.html
This page was last updated Tuesday, April 29, 2008.

Libraries & Collections | How Do I...? | Hours | Catalog | E-Research Tools | E-Journal Finder | Need Help?

DISTANCE EDUCATION
LIBRARY SERVICES

Requesting Materials: Document Delivery Services for Distance Education Students, Faculty, and Researchers at a Distance

Distance Education Students and Faculty

Distance education students and faculty who do not live in Chapel Hill or Carrboro may request delivery of books and photocopied articles from UNC-Chapel Hill or other locations. To request materials, you must register for the Interlibrary Loan Borrowing (ILB) Service. Log on with your UNC Onyen and password and complete the first-time user registration form. On the registration form choose DISTANCE EDUCATION as your "Status."

When completing the request form, enter the course number in the Additional Notes field. For example, "Carolina Courses Online: Art31."

Books are mailed to you via the U.S. postal service and return postage is included. Photocopies are delivered electronically to your ILB account. Materials requested from other libraries will take longer to obtain, so please be sure to enter the date by which you need the item to allow sufficient time. There is no charge for this document delivery service.

Books will be checked out to your account and must be received by the ILB Office by the due date in order to avoid late fines. Books that have no renewal restrictions may be renewed online through your ILB account. Please renew books two to three days before they are due.

Researchers at a Distance

Currently enrolled UNC students and current faculty, who are researching at a distance from Chapel Hill (both nationally and internationally), may request materials from UNC-Chapel Hill. To request materials, you must register for the Interlibrary Loan Borrowing (ILB) Service. Log on with your UNC Onyen and password and complete the first-time user registration form.

When completing the request form, be sure to note in the Additional Notes field that you are researching at a distance.

Books are mailed only within the contiguous United States via the U.S. Postal Service. Books will be checked out to your account and must be received by the ILB Office by the due date in order to avoid late fines. Books that have no renewal restrictions may be renewed online through your ILB account. Please renew books two to three days before they are due. There is no charge for this document delivery service.

Home | Hours | Search This Site | UNC Home

Website comments or questions: Library Web Team
Suggestions on Library Services? Give us your feedback.
URL: http://www.lib.unc.edu/de/doc_delivery.html
This page was last updated Wednesday, January 16, 2008.

Study Abroad Tutorials

Welcome! These tutorials are designed to introduce you to information resources you can use to research your destination country as well as tips for conducting research while you're abroad.

China	Italy
Czech Republic	Russia
France	South Africa
Mexico	Spain
India	United Kingdom

We'd love your feedback. **Recommend a country** or **share a research tip** of your own from a country you've visited.

Instructional Services | Library Tutorials Home | Contact Us | Library Home

Last updated: 03_05_2007

Study Abroad in China Research Tutorial
The University of North Carolina at Chapel Hill Libraries

1. Introduction
2. Getting to know China
3. Conducting Research in China
4. Accessing UNC's Resources While Abroad

About this Tutorial | Using this Tutorial | Site Map | Contact Us | Library Tutorials Home | Library Home

Last updated: 08_09_2007

China Study Abroad Research Tutorial

Introduction | Getting to Know China | Conducting Research in China | Accessing UNC's Resources Abroad

Research in China

Overview
Library Classification Systems
Academic Libraries
Public Libraries
Internet Cafés

Questions?

HELLO

UNDERGRADREF

IM Us!

Academic Libraries in China

Many colleges and universities across China maintain large libraries. Some things about the libraries will seem very familiar to you, and others may surprise you. UNC's Study Abroad Office encourages students to choose their study abroad experiences from its list of approved programs. Because of the large number and variety of libraries in China, this tutorial is tailored toward the libraries and other information resources UNC students will likely use in these programs. However, the skills you use in this tutorial will help you learn to navigate information resources as well.

Resources that you find in Chinese university libraries are similar to those at UNC-Chapel Hill's libraries. For example, numerous UNC students have studied at Chinese University of Hong Kong, and have found its library quite similar to UNC's. If you look at its Web page, you will see links to the catalog, e-journals, many of the same databases that you have used at UNC, and the same MyLibrary system that you can use to view your library account.

You may encounter many differences from UNC-Chapel Hill's libraries, especially if you are studying in mainland China. For instance, you may only be allowed to have a small number of books at once, or you may have to ask a librarian to give you certain materials. It's a good idea to read your university library's rules thoroughly before you go for the first time. Don't hesitate to contact UNC's librarians or ask a librarian at the library you're visiting for help! If you have more in-depth questions, you can contact the Libraries' Chinese-language specialist, Hsi-Chu Bolick.

<< back | next >>

About this Tutorial | Using this Tutorial | Site Map | Contact Us | Library Tutorials Home | Library Home

Last updated: 08_09_2007

http://www.lib.unc.edu/instruct/studyabroad/china/accessing/

China Study Abroad Research Tutorial

Introduction | Getting to Know China | Conducting Research in China | Accessing UNC's Resources Abroad

Using UNC Abroad

Overview
UNC-CH Libraries Web site
Articles
Specific Databases
Happy Travels

Questions?
HELLO
UNDERGRADREF
IM Us!

Accessing Resources at UNC

Many of the same information resources you relied on in Chapel Hill are available when you are conducting research abroad.

In this section you will learn about:

- How to access the libraries' Web resources abroad
- UNC resources you may find useful while studying abroad

<< back | next >>

About this Tutorial | Using this Tutorial | Site Map | Contact Us | Library Tutorials Home | Library Home

Last updated: 08_09_2007

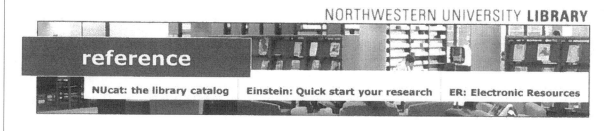

find   services   research assistance   about   help

Using Electronic Resources for Study Abroad Research

Ask Us
Call
Chat
Consult
Drop In
E-mail
Other Reference Desks at NUL
Subject Specialists at NUL

Reference Resources
Catalogs of Other Libraries
Guides and Handouts
Dictionaries, Encyclopedias & More

Instructional Services
Instruction Class Pages
Instruction Request Forms
Research Consultations
Tours
Workshops

More Services
EndNote Support
Mediated Online Searches
RefWorks Support
Research at Other Libraries

About the Reference Department
InfoCommons
Periodicals & Newspaper Reading Room
Reference Room
Reference Staff

Study Abroad Research Program (SARP)

Look for Information on a Topic

Don't know where to start? Northwestern subscribes to several hundred journal article databases.
Selected General Databases
🅝 Academic Search Premier [lots of full-text articles]
🅝 Expanded Academic Index [lots of full-text articles]
🅝 LexisNexis Academic [full-text newspapers, many foreign newspapers]
🅝 Factiva [similar to LexisNexis but not as fragmented]
🅝 JSTOR [full text of high quality journals, "moving wall" means **latest 3-5 years are NOT included**]
Find other general databases.

Fishing expeditions

Journal article databases allow you to perform complex searches within a limited scope of material. Einstein QuickStart and Google Scholar are two tools that let you search very broadly but with less precision. This can be helpful early in the research process. Be sure to **set your preferences in Google Scholar** so you can link to NU resources.

Use specialized databases to find material that is in research periodicals. Remember, Not all database have full text of the articles they index. Use the **Find it @ NU** *button to find the full article.*

Finding Books

Use **NUcat** (the online catalog) to identify books and **journal titles** that are available electronically. (Limit the search to **Location** Electronic Resources.) More on How to Find a Book

Selected Specialized Databases

Subject databases:

Business / Finance / Economics / Organizational Studies
N ABI/INFORM Global
N Business Source Premier
N EconLit
N SPORTDiscus
more

Family and Gender Studies
N Family & Society Studies Worldwide
N Gender Studies Database (includes *Men's Studies*, *Women's Studies International* and *Sexual Diversity Studies*)
N GenderWatch
more

Health and Medicine
N African HealthLine
N AIDSearch
N Medline
more

Law
N LexisNexis Academic Select "Legal" under "Easy Search" or "All Law Reviews" under "Power Search"

Political Science / Public Affairs
N CIAO: Columbia International Affairs Online
N PAIS International
N Worldwide Political Science Abstracts
more

Polling and Public Opinion
N Gallup Brain
N Polling the Nations

Religion
N ATLA
N Index Islamicus

Sociology / Anthropology
N Anthropology Plus Index to scholarly articles on anthropology, ethnology, archaeology and cultural studies.
N Anthrosource Fulltext articles from journals published by the American Anthropological Association
N International Bibliography of the Social Sciences
N Sociological Abstracts

Statistics
N LexisNexis Statistical
More statistics resources

Area studies:

Africa
N AllAfrica.com **African News Sources**
N International Index to Black Periodicals Full Text
N Sabinet Online
more

Latin America
N HLAS Online: Handbook of Latin American Studies
N Latinnews.com

Find other databases by subject.

Take a look at the **Research Guides A-Z** prepared by the Library's subject specialists.

Using Databases outside the Library

Most of the Library's databases are restricted to members of the NU community. When you are outside the Library, whether across the street or halfway around the world, you will need to authenticate yourself before you can use the databases. When you connect from the Library's website, you will be prompted for your **NetID** and **password** and passed through to the resource.

Additional Resources

Government Information and Publications
The Government and Geographic Information and Data Services is a depository library for U.S. government, State of Illinois, United Nations, Organization of American States, European Union, and World Tourism Organization publications in all formats. Visit the department before you leave to get statistics, policy documents, or other material that will be helpful in your research at this side. Their webpage also includes links to foreign government sites.

Foreign Newspapers
Get acquainted with your country before you leave! The Periodicals & Newspapers Reading Room has several newspapers from other countries that you can browse. You can also read newspapers of the country through any of the following sources:

N Global NewsBank
N LexisNexis Academic
N Newspaper Source

Country Information

Reference Sources

N *Annual Reviews*

N *Berkshire Encyclopedia of World History*. Gale Virtual Reference Library. Great Barrington, Mass.,: Berkshire Publishing Group, 2005.

N *Cities of the World*. Detroit, Mich.: Gale Research Co., 2002.

N *Countries and their cultures.* New York: Macmillan Reference USA, 2001.
MAIN Reference (Non-circulating) 306.03 C855

N *Encyclopedia of Anthropology*. Thousand Oaks, Calif.: Sage, 2006.
MAIN Reference (Encyclopedia case) (Non-circulating) 301.03 E557

Encyclopedia of Folk Medicine : Old World and New World Traditions. Santa Barbara, Calif.: Abc-Clio, 2004.
MAIN Reference (Non-circulating) 615.8803 H362e

N *Encyclopedia of Human Development.* Thousand Oaks, Calif.: Sage Publications, 2006.
MAIN Reference (Non-circulating) 155.03 E56

Encyclopedia of International Development. London ; New York: Routledge, 2005.
MAIN Reference (Non-circulating) 338.9003 E56

N *Encyclopedia of Islam and the Muslim World.* New York: Macmillan Reference USA : Thomson/Gale, 2004.
MAIN Reference (Non-circulating) 909.09767 E56

N *Encyclopedia of Religion*
MAIN Reference (Encyclopedia case)
Call number: 200.321 E56 2005

N *Encyclopedia of Sociology*. 2nd ed. New York: Macmillan Reference USA, 2000.
MAIN Reference (Encyclopedia case) (Non-circulating) 301.03 E565 2000
MAIN Core (Reference) 301.03 E565 2000
SCHAFFNER Reference (Non-circulating) 301.03 E565

2000

🅽 *Encyclopedia of the Modern Middle East and North Africa.* 2nd ed. Detroit, Mich.: Macmillan Reference USA, 2004.
MAIN Reference (Non-circulating) 956.003 E56 2004

🅽 *Encyclopedia of world cultures.* Boston, Mass.: G.K. Hall, 1991.
MAIN Reference (Non-circulating) 306.03 E56

🅽 *Encyclopedia of World Poverty.* Thousand Oaks, Calif.: SAGE Publications, 2006.
MAIN Reference (Non-circulating) 362.503 E56

The Greenwood Encyclopedia of Women's Issues Worldwide. Westport, Conn.: Greenwood Press, 2003.
MAIN Reference (Non-circulating) 305.403 G8157

Handbook of research design & social measurement. 6th ed. Thousand Oaks, Calif.: Sage Publications, 2002.
MAIN Library 302.072 M647h

Handbook of social theory. Thousands Oaks, CA: Sage, 2001.
MAIN Reference (Non-circulating) 301.01 H236

🅽 *International Encyclopedia of Marriage and Family.* 2nd ed. New York: Macmillan Reference USA, 2003.
MAIN Reference (Non-circulating) 306.803 E56 2003

Putting it all together

Cite your material in a standard format

APA Style (An online guide from Purdue University Online Writing Lab (OWL))
The complete APA style manual, officially called **Publication manual of the American Psychological Association,** 5th edition, 2001 is located at the Reference Desk at call number 029.6 A513p 2001

MLA Style (An online guide from Purdue University Online Writing Lab (OWL))
The **MLA Handbook for Writers of Research Papers**, 6th edition, 2003 is located at the Reference Desk at call number 808.02 M685 2003

🅽 Chicago Manual of Style, 15th edition, 2003, is available online or in the Reference Room and Core at call number 655.2 C53 2003

Turabian, a version of the *Chicago Manual of Style* geared toward writers of term papers. The 6th edition, *A Manual for Writers of Term Papers, Theses, and Dissertations* by Kate L. Turabian, is located at call number 029.6 T929m 1996 at the Reference Desk.

Bibliographic Software

EndNote is a software program that helps you keep track of your reading. You can store information about books and articles so you can find them again when you need them. It also works with Microsoft Word to automatically format citations, footnotes and bibliographies.

For more information check the EndNote support page.

Need Help? Ask a librarian

If something doesn't work right, or if you can't find what you need, get in touch with the Reference Librarians.
Call us at 847-491-7656
E-mail us at refdept@northwestern.edu
or connect with us real-time through Answers Online or IM

Take advantage of a Research Consultations--meet with a librarian one on one for personalized, in-depth help.

Scott Garton
Reference Librarian
Email: s-garton@northwestern.edu
Office phone: 847.491.3825
Reference desk phone: 847.491.7656

refdept@northwestern.edu

NORTHWESTERN
UNIVERSITY

Search the Library web site [   ] [Search ▶]

ALICE | InfoTree | home

ASK A LIBRARIAN ▶ im | chat | phone | e-mail

| Find | Services | Collections | Library Info |

Off-Campus Services

Troubleshooting

Quick Reference Guide (PDF)

Electronic Resources

Distance Education Blog

Plagiarism Websites

How-to Guides

Contact Info

Services for Off-Campus Patrons

Welcome to Ohio University Libraries. We have a number of resources available to our off-campus users. The links on the left will give you some basic places to start—with the focus on electronic resources (databases, websites, reference guides) that are available to you at any time. Remember, you must be enrolled in an Ohio University campus-based course or member of the university faculty or staff to access some databases.

For your research needs, we have created InfoTree . This is our gateway to resources (both print and electronic) organized by discipline. It has many full-text databases and other resources accessible from off-campus locations.

Thousands of individual electronic books and journals, which you can connect to from off-campus, are listed in ALICE, our online catalog.

And, of course, please visit the University Libraries homepage and let us know if you have any questions or suggestions!

Archives & Special Collections | International Collections | Health Sciences | Music & Dance

OHIO University Libraries
Athens, OH 45701-2978
Phone: (740) 593-2699

Last updated: February 27, 2008
This page is maintained by Marne Grinolds.
Please use our Feedback Form for your questions, comments, and suggestions about the Libraries' services and resources.

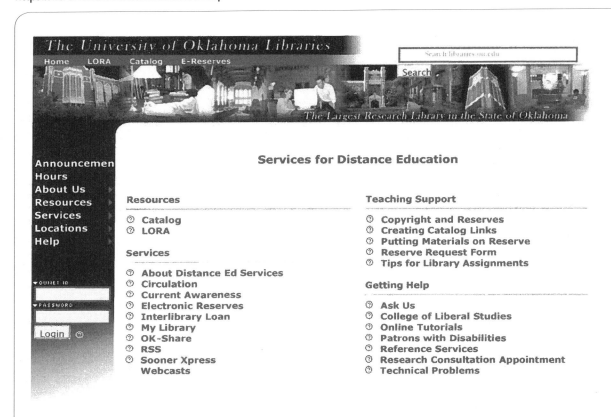

Services for Distance Education

Resources

- ⑦ Catalog
- ⑦ LORA

Services

- ⑦ About Distance Ed Services
- ⑦ Circulation
- ⑦ Current Awareness
- ⑦ Electronic Reserves
- ⑦ Interlibrary Loan
- ⑦ My Library
- ⑦ OK-Share
- ⑦ RSS
- ⑦ Sooner Xpress
- Webcasts

Teaching Support

- ⑦ Copyright and Reserves
- ⑦ Creating Catalog Links
- ⑦ Putting Materials on Reserve
- ⑦ Reserve Request Form
- ⑦ Tips for Library Assignments

Getting Help

- ⑦ Ask Us
- ⑦ College of Liberal Studies
- ⑦ Online Tutorials
- ⑦ Patrons with Disabilities
- ⑦ Reference Services
- ⑦ Research Consultation Appointment
- ⑦ Technical Problems

Contact Us   Employment   About this Site   Other Libraries

Disclaimer
Copyright

R S S   PODCASTS

401 W Brooks Street
Norman, OK 73019
(405) 325-4142

OKLAHOMA STATE UNIVERSITY: Digital Library Services

http://www.library.okstate.edu/dls/index.htm

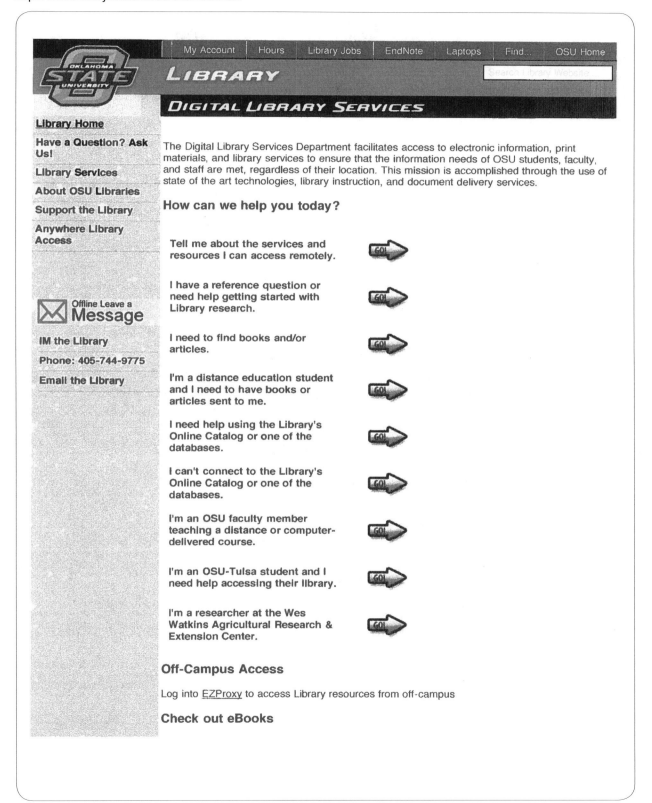

We offer access to over 14,000 Electronic Books via
More details and registration information

Contact DLS

Staff
Robin Leech, Digital Initiatives Head
Roy Degler, Librarian
Brandon Boyles, Senior Library Technician 1

Phone & Email
Telephone: 405-744-9161
Toll-free: 877-744-9161
FAX: 405-744-7579
Email: lib-dls@okstate.edu

Mailing Address
Digital Library Services
Edmon Low Library
Oklahoma State University
Stillwater, OK 74078-1071

Hours • Anywhere Library Access • EZProxy • Renew Online • Search This Site • OSU Home • Comments

URL: http://www.library.okstate.edu/dls/index.htm
Last Updated: 1 May 2008

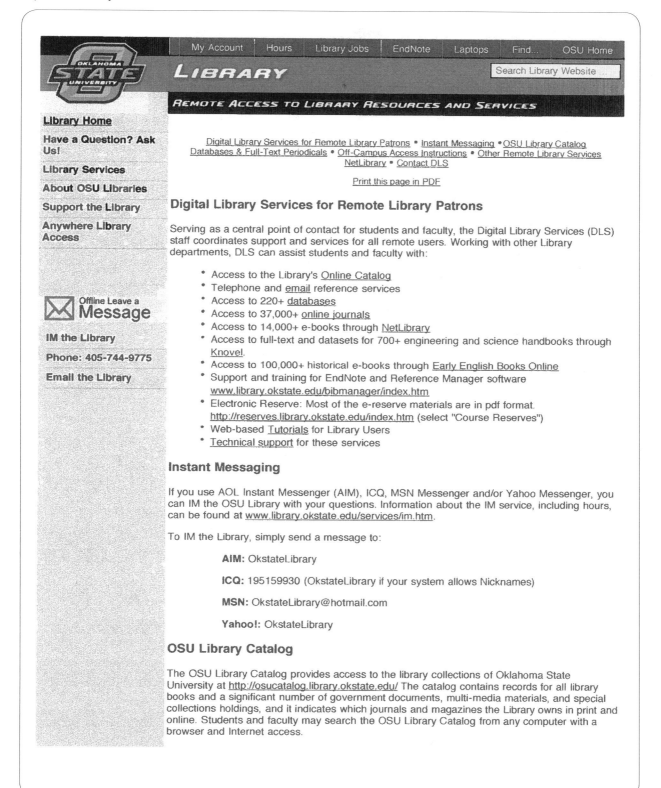

To view a list of items you've checked out or to renew items, click on "My Account" on the Library's home page (www.library.okstate.edu) or in the catalog.

Databases & Full-Text Journals

The OSU library provides access to over 220 Web-based resources, including databases of journal, magazine and newspaper articles (many with full-text), as well as online dictionaries, almanacs and other reference works. A list of the Web-based resources can be found at www.library.okstate.edu/database/. For current OSU students, faculty, and staff, access to these resources is available from any Internet-connected computer on campus, or by logging in from off-campus. Those resources available to the non-OSU community are indicated with a globe icon (🌐).

A list of over 37,000 current full-text journals, newspapers and magazines may be found by clicking "Full-Text Journals" on the OSU Library Homepage (or www.library.okstate.edu/ftbd/index.htm). Each title is linked to the corresponding database which houses full-text access.

Off-Campus Access Instructions

The OSU Library offers off-campus access to students, faculty, and staff to online journals, indexes, and databases. More information and off-campus access instructions may be found on the web at www.library.okstate.edu/dls/ezproxy.htm.

Other Remote Library Services

The OSU Library offers a variety of Web-based services. Links to the online forms may also be found on the "Services" page www.library.okstate.edu/services.htm.

* Ask Us a Question (E-mail Reference)
* Article & Book Requests (Interlibrary Services)
* Request a Book or Article from the Annex
* Request a Book With a Status of "In Process"
* Recall Books
* Suggest a Book for Purchase
* Ask Circulation Questions

NetLibrary

NetLibrary is an Internet-based electronic library offering e-books for use OSU students, faculty, and staff. E-Books are electronic versions of printed books which may be viewed from any computer connected to the Internet. OSU currently has access to 10,000+ copyrighted books and 3,500 public domain titles.

Contact DLS

Staff
Robin Leech, Digital Initiatives Head
Roy Degler, Librarian
Brandon Boyles, Senior Library Technician 1

Phone & Email
Telephone: 405-744-9161
Toll-free: 877-744-9161
FAX: 405-744-7579
Email: lib-dls@okstate.edu

Mailing Address
Digital Library Services
Edmon Low Library

Where academic excellence meets cultural diversity

SUF

Syracuse University in Florence

About SUF | Academics | Academic Resources | Student Life | Featured Events | Publications | Community Engagement

Library

ACADEMIC RESOURCES

Library

Media Lab

Technology Resources

Writing Center

SUF's expanding collection of over 12,000 items is one of the largest of any US study abroad program in Italy. Books, videos and journals are carefully chosen around the curriculum, ensuring that students find the most important resources for their studies right on the SUF campus. Books may be checked out for use off campus.

The library offers students attractive study and consultation areas on two floors, wireless internet access, temporary lockers and a card-operated photocopier.

SUF Library Staff:
Librarian **Tom Dodd** (tcdodd@syr.fi.it) received his Post-Graduate degree from the College of Librarianship, Wales. He is a Chartered Member of the UK Library Association.

Circulation Manager **Carol Ann Estall** (caestall@syr.fi.it) has worked in SUF's library since 1993. She is very familiar with the collection, and welcomes the challenge of helping students with difficult research projects.

Library Assistant **Elena Gavilli** (eegavill@syr.fi.it) received her degree in Foreign Languages and Literature at the Faculty of Arts at the University of Florence. She has also recently completed a course in Library Science.

Useful Links:

* SUF Library Catalog

* Syracuse University Bird Library

* Biblioteca Nazionale Centrale di Firenze

* Biblioteca di scienze tecnologiche. Architettura

* IRS01 Library

Opening hours

Mon. - Thurs. 8:45 - 8pm
Fri. 9 - 2pm
Sat. closed
Sun. 12 - 9pm
Extended hours during mid-term and final exams.

Students in film classes can use the library's resources to re-watch a movie.

"Loved the librarians."

"The viewing room upstairs is awesome!"

"The librarians were very helpful!"

"Nice environment to work in."

"I enjoyed the small study rooms. The lighting was perfect."

"Beautiful!"

"I can't think of any changes, it was nicely run."

"Library staff = amazing!"

Libraries — TEXAS TECH UNIVERSITY

University Library | Architecture | Southwest Collection

RESEARCH
Online Catalog
Journals/Periodicals
e-Journal Search
Find-it-Fast
Find Articles
e-Books
Ask a Librarian
Subject Resources
Govt Documents/Maps
Theses and Dissertations
Digital Collections
3D Animation Lab
Area Libraries
Other TTU Collections

SERVICES
Borrowing
Document Delivery
Log In to ILLiad
Instruction/Tours
Distance Learning
Course/E-Reserve
Syllabi
Digital Media Studio

ABOUT
Employment
Help/FAQs
Staff Directory
Hours
Online Forms
Mission/Values

GIVE TO LIBRARIES
Give Online
Coach Knight Fund

COMPUTING
Workstations/Software
Wireless
VPN Help
Computer Help
TTU Student
Technology Services

ATLC TLTC

Printing Copying

SITEMAP

Set Text Size: A A A

Distance Learning Services @ TTU Libraries

Welcome to Texas Tech University Libraries where your success is our business! We are dedicated to providing our Distance Learners with the same service and satisfaction our on-campus users receive. Here you'll find library resources to help you achieve all of your educational endeavors. Remember we're committed to your success at Texas Tech. Have a great semester!

Services for Students   **Services for Faculty**

Contact Information

Please feel free to contact the Distance Learning Committee members directly and/or use the toll free telephone number, 1-888-270-3369:

Donell Callender	donell.callender@ttu.edu	(806) 742-2239 x331
Barbara McArthur	barbara.mcarthur@ttu.edu	(806) 742-2249 x221
Jake Syma	jake.syma@ttu.edu	(806) 742-2238 x282

- **Toll Free:** 1-888-270-3369
- **Email and Chat:** http://library.ttu.edu/ul/help/ask/
- **Fax:** (806) 742-1964 (Reference / Government Documents), (806) 742-1920 (Document Delivery).
- **Mail:** Texas Tech University Library, 18th St. and Boston Ave., PO Box 40002, Lubbock, TX 79409-0002
- For more telephone numbers and email addresses, click here.

TTU Libraries are not responsible for the content of external sources. For questions about this page, contact Jake Syma, Social Sciences Librarian.
[v] (806) 742.2238 x282
[f] (806) 742.1964
[e] jake.syma@ttu.edu

This page last modified on 16 Nov 2005, 11:30.

University Library | Architecture | Southwest Collection

RESEARCH
Online Catalog
Journals/Periodicals
e-Journal Search
Find-it-Fast
Find Articles
e-Books
Ask a Librarian
Subject Resources
Govt Documents/Maps
Theses and Dissertations
Digital Collections
3D Animation Lab
Area Libraries
Other TTU Collections

SERVICES
Borrowing
Document Delivery
Log In to ILLiad
Instruction/Tours
Distance Learning
Course/E-Reserve
Syllabi
Digital Media Studio

ABOUT
Employment
Help/FAQs
Staff Directory
Hours
Online Forms
Mission/Values

GIVE TO LIBRARIES
Give Online
Coach Knight Fund

COMPUTING
Workstations/Software
Wireless
VPN Help
Computer Help
TTU Student
Technology Services
ATLC   TLTC
Printing   Copying

SITEMAP

Set Text Size: A A A

Distance Learning

Distance Services for Students

- Connecting from Off-Campus

- Obtaining Materials
  (Books, Journals, Magazines, ...)

- Need an Item Delivered to You?

- Course/E-Reserve

- Library Instruction

- We Want to Hear from You

- Contact Us

TTU Libraries are not responsible for the content of external sources. For questions about this page, contact Jake Syma, Social Sciences Librarian.
[v] (806) 742.2238 x282
[f] (806) 742.1964
[e] jake.syma@ttu.edu

This page last modified on 7 Dec 2005, 11:14.

TEXAS TECH UNIVERSITY: Distance Learning. Delivery of Materials

http://library.ttu.edu/dlservices/delivery.php

Libraries — TEXAS TECH UNIVERSITY

University Library | Architecture | Southwest Collection

RESEARCH
Online Catalog
Journals/Periodicals
e-Journal Search
Find-it-Fast
Find Articles
e-Books
Ask a Librarian
Subject Resources
Govt Documents/Maps
Theses and Dissertations
Digital Collections
3D Animation Lab
Area Libraries
Other TTU Collections

SERVICES
Borrowing
Document Delivery
Log In to ILLiad
Instruction/Tours
Distance Learning
Course/E-Reserve
Syllabi
Digital Media Studio

ABOUT
Employment
Help/FAQs
Staff Directory
Hours
Online Forms
Mission/Values

GIVE TO LIBRARIES
Give Online
Coach Knight Fund

COMPUTING
Workstations/Software
Wireless
VPN Help
Computer Help
TTU Student
Technology Services
ATLC TLTC
Printing Copying

SITEMAP

Set Text Size: A A A

Distance Learning

Delivery of Materials

TTU Libraries provides access and delivery of materials (books, articles, multimedia, etc.) to distance students. Many books, articles, and government documents are available electronically and can be accessed online. Please check the "Obtaining Materials " Webpage to determine if the item is available online. The table below summerizes the delivery options for a variety of materials.

Material	Delivery	Form/Contact	Cost
Books Videos DVD's (Owned by TTU Libraries)	Mailed (FedEx ground) to patron at no cost. The patron is responsible for returning the item to TTU Libraries.	The item is requested through Document Delivery via a Form: http://library.ttu.edu/ul/dd/ Groups of citations can be sent to: libraries.docdel@ttu.edu	No cost for delivery, but the patron is responsible for returning the book
Articles/Copies	Scanned and sent to Web Server. Patron gets email about link and password.	same as books	No cost.

TTU Libraries are not responsible for the content of external sources. For questions about this page, contact Donell Callender, Humanities Librarian.
[v] (806) 742-2238 x267
[f] (806) 742-1964
[e] donell.callender@ttu.edu

This page last modified on 21 Nov 2005, 14:46

SELECTED RESOURCES

DOCUMENTS

ACRL Distance Learning Section. *Library Services for Distance Learning: The Fourth Bibliography.* 2008. http://libraryservicesdistancelearning.oaktonlibrary.wikispaces.net/

Bonnette, Ashley. "Voyage of Discovery: Around the World with Semester at Sea." *Louisiana Libraries* 68, no. 2 (Fall 2005): 9–12.

Brogan, Martha L. "Trends in International Education: New Imperatives in Academic Librarianship." *College and Research Libraries* 51, no. 3 (May 1990): 196–206.

Brown, Sally, and Elspeth Jones. *Internationalising Higher Education.* London; New York: Routledge, 2007.

Burn, Barbara B. *Integrating Study Abroad into the Undergraduate Liberal Arts Curriculum: Eight Institutional Case Studies.* Contributions to the Study of Education 44. New York: Greenwood Press, 1991.

Byram, Michael, and Anwei Feng. *Living and Studying Abroad: Research and Practice.* Languages for Intercultural Communication and Education 12. Clevedon England; Buffalo, NY: Multilingual Matters Ltd., 2006.

Byram, Michael, Adam Nichols, and David Stevens. *Developing Intercultural Competence in Practice.* Languages for Intercultural Communication and Education 1. Clevedon, England; Buffalo, NY: Multilingual Matters, 2001.

Carlson, Jerry S., and Study Abroad Evaluation Project. *Study Abroad: The Experience of American Undergraduates.* Contributions to the Study of Education 37. New York: Greenwood Press, 1990.

Chakraborty, Mou, and Johanna Tunon. "Taking the Distance Out of Library Services Offered to International Graduate Students: Considerations, Challenges, and Concerns." *Journal of Library Administration* 37, no. 1/2 (2002): 163–76.

Comparative Education Research Centre, Meeri Hellstén, and Peter Ninnes. *Internationalizing Higher Education: Critical Explorations of Pedagogy and Policy.* CERC Studies in Comparative Education 16. Hong Kong: Comparative Education Research Centre, University of Hong Kong; Kluwer Academic, 2005.

Engeldinger, Eugene A. "Bibliographic Instruction for Study Abroad Programs." *College & Research Libraries News* 46, no. 8 (September 1985): 395–98.

Goodson, Carol F. *Providing Library Services for Distance Education Students: A How-to-do-it Manual*. How-to-do-it Manuals for Libraries 108. New York: Neal-Schuman Publishers, 2001.

Gutek, Gerald Lee. *American Education in a Global Society: Internationalizing Teacher Education*. White Plains, NY: Longman, 1992.

Hoffa, William, and Forum on Education Abroad. *A History of US Study Abroad: Beginnings to 1965*. Carlisle, PA: Forum on Education Abroad, 2007.

Lee, Janet. "A Voyage of Discovery: The Semester at Sea Experience." *Colorado Libraries* 30, no. 1 (Spring 2004): 4–8.

Miller, William, and Rita M. Pellen. *Internet Reference Support for Distance Learners*. Binghamton, NY: Haworth Information Press, 2004.

Mizzy, Danianne. "Around the World in 100 Days." *College & Research Libraries News* 63, no. 10 (November 2002): 716–17.

Popa, Opritsa D., and Sandra J. Lamprecht. *Directory of Selected University Libraries Most Frequently Used by University of California Students Studying Abroad*, 1990.

Robalik, Heather Anne. *Study Abroad: An Exploration of Student Development and Student Perceptions*. Gainesville, Fla.: University of Florida, 2006.

Sims, Serbrenia J. *Student Outcomes Assessment: A Historical Review and Guide to Program Development*. Contributions to the Study of Education 52. New York: Greenwood Press, 1992.

Stallings, Dees. "Pros and Cons of Partnering: A Vcampus Perspective." *The Journal of Academic Librarianship* 27, no. 1 (January 2001): 52–56.

Swinger, Alice K. *Planning for Study Abroad*. Fastback 228. Bloomington, Ind.: Phi Delta Kappa Educational Foundation, 1985.

United States Congress House Committee on Foreign Affairs. *Senator Paul Simon Study Abroad Foundation Act of 2007: Report (to accompany H.R. 1469) (including cost estimate of the Congressional Budget Office)*. United States Congress House Report 110-138. Washington, DC: US GPO, 2007.

United States Congress Senate Committee on Foreign Relations. *Senator Paul Simon Study Abroad Foundation Act: Report (to accompany H.R. 1469)*. United States Congress Senate Report 110-272. Washington, DC: US GPO, 2008.

Vestal, Theodore M. *International Education: Its History and Promise for Today*. Westport, Conn.: Praeger, 1994.

Walker, G. R. *Educating the Global Citizen*. Saxmundham, UK: John Catt Educational, 2006.

SPEC KIT TITLE LIST

SPEC KIT PRICE INFORMATION

Individual Kits: $35 ARL members/$45 nonmembers, plus shipping and handling.

Individual issues of the Transforming Libraries (TL) subseries: $28, plus shipping and handling.

SHIPPING & HANDLING

U.S.: UPS Ground delivery, $10 per publication. Canada: UPS Ground delivery, $15 per publication

International and rush orders: Call or e-mail for quote.

PAYMENT INFORMATION

Make check or money order payable in U.S. funds to the ASSOCIATION OF RESEARCH LIBRARIES, Federal ID #52-0784198-N. MasterCard and Visa accepted.

SEND ORDERS TO: ARL Publications Distribution Center, P.O. Box 531, Annapolis Junction, MD 20701-0531
phone (301) 362-8196; fax (301) 206-9789; e-mail pubs@arl.org

ORDER ONLINE AT: http://www.arl.org/resources/pubs/index.shtml